Letters

from the

Hinterland:

2018:

a Coming Reckoning

Max Laszlo

Dedication

For my Family …

Where it all began …

With the ancient Magyars …

I am forever in your debt …

And you are forever in my thanks … …

Contents	Page

Historian's Note

I am an immigrant. I am an immigrant with Hungarian-Germanic roots reaching back to the Crusades. At 18 months of age, with family, after waiting for 5 years, I came to America in March of 1957. I am an immigrant who matter-of-factly was offered life, liberty, and the pursuit of happiness. Nothing more. But that was worth infinitely more than anything. I can no longer say nothing less, since in many ways on many days over many years slices of the pie have been sold or stolen or thrown into city dumps. Life, liberty, and the Pursuit of Happiness are forced, by New World Order tuxedoed goons and intellectual buffoons, with fool's gold spoons, to kneel at feet of death. My family and friends helped build the industrial heartland in Detroit, Dearborn, Cleveland, Toledo, Gary, Moline, Chicago, and Milwaukee; at a time when Samson-like Smokestack America had not yet been incinerated, by New World Order and Deep State orderlies and disorderlies and borderlesslies, into dust and ash and trash and dishonored and humiliated hinterland. It did not begin with Puppet Pelosi. It did not begin with Mule Mueller. And it did not begin with Queen Hillary Artillery and her boneheaded jackbooted buffoon, Bill. Yes, almost forever here and there and everywhere have we been owned and loaned and controlled by that that deplorable and despicable deep state. To this day, I can still see and hear perverted priests lecture me that, in 1960, Dummycrat (somehow not such dummies during momentous moments) Chicago Mayor Richard Daley's treasonous theft of Illinois for JFK over Nixon was, in the eyes of God, both moral and noble (God somehow is sometimes not only cross-eyed but also scatter-brained). To this day, I can still see and hear the fake media empires ledby Walter Crackpot Pinkster Cronkite (for CBS, the CNN of the 50s 60s), lecture me that the needs of the Nation, meaning United Nations, necessitated the assist from LBJ's steer manure machine in Texas for a permanent melting pot (more accurately witch's brew crockpot) for the illegal, immoral, impeachment-mandating Putridencies, er, Presidencies, of JFK and LBJ. To this day, I can still see and hear my university professors lecture me through beer and weed how democracy had demanded the dead in Chicago and Dallas needed to rise up from their graves, and to vote, both early and often. Yes, the New World Order's and Deep State's mutation of the abomination between Jim Crow and Karl Marx had conquered an entire planet, a long, long time ago, and not in a galaxy far, far away. Until our Father in Heaven decides that this historian's work is done, both in this life and on this earth, you will that this historian will always give the devils their due.

The new world order's warlords and druglords and slumlords and overlords ...
And foaming at the mouth fake Lords ...

Slicing my vocal cords and carving my site and digging my grave ...
For centuries ...

And cutting the cedars and raising the hammers and aiming the iron nails ...
In brutal iron fists ...

But they could not anticipate ...
That vast expanding resurrecting Hinterland ...

And they could not anticipate ...
A Coming Reckoning ... ...

Foundations

But when ye pray, use not vain repetitions, as the heathen DO: for they think that they shall be heard for their much speaking. Be not ye therefore like unto them: for your Father knoweth what things ye have ned of, before ye ask him. After this manner therefore pray ye:
Our Father which art in heaven, Hallowed be thy name. Thy kingdom come, Thy will be done in earth, as IT IS in heaven. Give us this day our daily bread. And forgive us our debts, as we forgive our debtors. And lead us not into temptation, but deliver us from evil: For thine is the kingdom, and the power, and the glory, forever. Amen. For if ye forgive men their trespasses, your heavenly Father will also forgive you: But if ye forgive not men their trespasses, neither will your Father forgive your trespasses.

Matthew 6: 7-15
King James Version (KJV)

Then said Jesus to them again, Peace *be* unto you: as *my* Father hath sent me, even so send I you. And when he had said this, he breathed on *them*, and saith unto them, Receive ye the Holy Ghost: Whose soever sins ye remit, they are remitted unto them; *and* whose soever *sins* ye retain, they are retained. But Thomas, one of the twelve, called Didymus, was not with them when Jesus came. The other disciples therefore said unto him, We have seen the Lord. But he said unto them, Except I shall see in his hands the print of the nails, and put my finger into the print of the nails, and thrust my hand into his side, I will not believe. And after eight days again his disciples were within, and Thomas with them: *then* came Jesus, the doors being shut, and stood in the midst, and said, Peace *be* unto you. Then saith he to Thomas, Reach hither thy finger, and behold my hands; and reach hither thy hand, and thrust *it* into my side: and be not faithless, but believing. And Thomas answered and said unto him, My Lord and my God. Jesus saith unto him, Thomas, because thou hast seen me, thou hast believed: blessed *are* they that have not seen, and *yet* have believed. And many other signs truly did Jesus in the presence of his disciples, which are not written in this book: But these are written, that ye might believe that Jesus is the Christ, the Son of God; and that believing ye might have life through his name.

John 20: 21-31
KJV

And God spake all these words, saying, I *am* the LORD thy God, which have brought thee out of the land of Egypt --- out of the house of bondage.

Thou shalt have no other gods before me.

Thou shalt not make unto thee any graven image, or any likeness *of any thing* that *is* in heaven above, or that *is* in the earth beneath, or that *is* in the water under the earth: Thou shalt not bow down thyself to them, nor serve them: for I the LORD thy God *am* a jealous God, visiting the iniquity of the fathers upon the children unto the third and fourth *generation* of them that hate me; And shewing mercy unto thousands of them that love me, and keep my commandments.

Thou shalt not take the name of the LORD thy God in vain; for the LORD will not hold him guiltless that taketh his name in vain.

Remember the Sabbath day, to keep it holy. Six days shalt thou labour, and do all thy work: But the Seventh day *is* the Sabbath of the LORD thy God: *in it* thou shalt not do any work, thou, nor thy son, nor thy daughter, nor thy manservant, nor thy maidservant, nor thy cattle, nor thy stranger that *is* within thy gates: For *in* six days the LORD made Heaven and earth, the sea, and all that in them *is*, and rested the Seventh day: wherefore the LORD blessed the Sabbath day, and hallowed it.

Honour thy father and thy mother: that thy days may be long upon the land which the LORD thy God giveth thee.

Thou shalt not kill.

Thou shalt not commit adultery.

Thou shalt not steal.

Thou shalt not bear false witness against thy neighbor.

Thou shalt not covet thy neighbour's house, thou shalt not covet thy neighbour's wife, nor his manservant, nor his maidservant, nor his ox, nor his ass, nor any thing that *is* thy neighbour's.

And all the people saw the thunderings, and the lightnings, and the noise of the trumpet, and the mountain smoking: and when the people saw *it*, they removed, and stood afar off. And they said unto Moses, Speak thou with us, and we will hear: but let not God speak with us, lest we die.

Exodus 20: 1-19

KJV

The Lord *is* my Shepherd; I shall not want. He maketh me to lie down in green pastures: He leadeth me beside the still waters. He restoreth my soul: He leadeth me in the paths of righteousness for His name's sake. Yea, though I walk through the valley of the shadow of death, I will fear no evil: for Thou *art* with me; Thy rod and Thy staff they comfort me. Thou prepares a table before me in the presence of mine enemies: Thou anointest my head with oil; my cup runneth over. Surely goodness and mercy shall follow me all the days of my life: and I will dwell in the house of the Lord for ever.

Psalm 23: 1-6

KJV

He that dwelleth in the secret place of the most High shall abide under the shadow of the Almighty. I will say of the LORD, *He is* my refuge and my fortress: my God; in him will I trust. Surely he shall deliver thee from the snare of the fowler, *and* from the noisome pestilence. He shall cover thee with his feathers, and under his wings shalt thou trust: his truth *shall be thy* shield and buckler. Thou shalt not be afraid for the terror by night; *nor* for the arrow *that* flieth by day; *Nor* for the pestilence *that* walketh in darkness; *nor* for the destruction *that* wasteth at noonday. A thousand shall fall at thy side, and ten thousand at thy right hand; *but* it shall not come nigh thee. Only with thine eyes shalt thou behold and see the reward of the wicked. Because thou hast made the LORD, *which is* my refuge, *even* the most High, thy habitation; There shall no evil befall thee, neither shall any plague come nigh thy dwelling. For he shall give his angels charge over thee, to keep thee in all thy ways. They shall bear thee up in *their* hands, lest thou dash thy foot against a stone. Thou shalt tread upon the lion and adder: the young lion and the dragon shalt thou trample under feet. Because he hath set his love upon me, therefore will I deliver him: I will set him on high, because he hath known my name. He shall call upon me, and I will answer him: I *will* be with him in trouble; I will deliver him, and honour him. With long life will I satisfy him, and shew him my salvation.

Psalm 91: 1-16

KJV

My son, forget not my law; but let thine heart keep my commandments: For length of days, and long life, and peace, shall they add to thee. Let not mercy and truth forsake thee: bind them about thy neck; write them upon the table of thine heart: So shalt thou find favour and good understanding in the sight of God and man. Trust in the LORD with all thine heart; and lean not unto thine own understanding. In all thy ways acknowledge him, and he shall direct thy paths. Be not wise in thine own eyes: fear the LORD, and depart from evil. It shall be health to thy navel, and marrow to thy bones. Honour the LORD with thy substance, and with the firstfruits of all thine increase: So shall thy barns be filled with plenty, and thy presses shall burst out with new wine. My son, despise not the chastening of the LORD; neither be weary of his correction: For whom the LORD loveth he correcteth; even as a father the son *in whom* he delighteth. Happy *is* the man *that* findeth wisdom, and the man *that* getteth understanding. For the merchandise of it *is* better than the merchandise of silver, and the gain thereof than fine gold. She *is* more precious than rubies: and all the things thou canst desire are not to be compared unto her. Length of days *is* in her right hand; *and* in her left hand riches and honour. Her ays *are* ways of pleasantness, and all her paths *are* peace. She *is* a tree of life to them that lay hold upon her: and happy *is every one* that retaineth her. The LORD by wisdom hath founded the earth; by understanding hath he established the heavens.

Proverbs 3: 1-19

KJV

To every *thing there is* a season, and a time to every purpose under the heaven:

A time to be born, and a time to die;
A time to plant, and a time to pluck up *that which is* planted;
A time to kill, and a time to heal;
A time to break down, and a time to build up;
A time to weep, and a time to laugh;
A time to mourn, and a time to dance;
A time to cast away stones, and a time to gather stones together;
A time to embrace, and a time to refrain from embracing;
A time to get, and a time to lose;
A time to keep, and a time to cast away;
A time to rend, and a time to sew;
A time to keep silence, and a time to speak;
A time to love, and a time to hate;
A time of war, and a time of peace.

Ecclesiastes 3: 1-22
JKV

I give and bequeath my soul to Almighty God, Who gave it to me, hoping that, through the meritorious death and passion of our Savior and Redeemer, Jesus Christ, to receive absolution and remission for all my sins.

… …

My soul I resign into the hands of my Almighty Creator, Whose tender mercies are all over His works, humbly hoping from His unbounded mercy and benevolence through the merits of my blessed Savior, a remission of my sins.

George Mason
Founding Father
"Father" of the Bill of Rights

In the colonies, we issue our own money. It is called Colonial Scrip. We issue it in proper proportion to the demands of trade and industry, to make the products pass easily from producers to consumers. In this manner, creating for ourselves our own paper money, we control its purchasing power, and we have no interest to pay to no one.

… …

The colonies would gladly have borne the little tax on tea and other matters had it not been that England took away from the colonies their money, which created unemployment and dissatisfaction. The inability of colonists to get power to issue their own money permanently, out of the hands of George III and international bankers --- was the prime reason for the Revolutionary War.

Benjamin Franklin
Founding Father
"Father" of the Constitution

It is our true policy to steer clear of permanent alliances with any portion of the foreign world; so far, I mean, as we are now at liberty to do it; for let me not be understood as capable of patronizing infidelity to existing engagements. I hold the maxim no less applicable to public than to private affairs, that honesty is always the best policy. I repeat it, therefore, let those engagements be observed in their genuine sense. But, in my opinion, it is unnecessary and would be unwise to extend them.

… …

However [political parties] may now and then answer popular ends, they are likely in the course of time and things, to become potent engines, by which cunning, ambitious, and unprincipled men will be enabled to subvert the power of the people and to usurp for themselves the reins of government, destroying afterwards the very engines which have lifted them to unjust dominion.

George Washington
Founding Father
1st U.S. President

Our constitution was made only for a moral and religious people. It is wholly inadequate to the government of any other.

… …

The general principles on which the fathers achieved independence were the general principles of Christianity. I will avow, that I then believed, and that I now believe, that those general principles of Christianity are as eternal and immutable as the existence and attributes of God.

John Adams
Founding Father
2nd U.S. President

I have sworn upon the altar of God, eternal hostility against every form of tyranny over the mind of man.

... ...

We hold these truths to be self-evident: that all men are created equal; that they are endowed by their Creator with certain unalienable rights; that among these are life, liberty, and the pursuit of happiness.

Thomas Jefferson
Founding Father
3rd U.S. President

A thorough knowledge of the Bible is worth more than a college education.

… …

What is true of creed is no less true of nationality. There is no room in this country for hyphenated Americanism. When I refer to hyphenated Americans, I do not refer to naturalized Americans. Some of the very best Americans I have ever known were naturalized Americans, Americans born abroad.

… …

The one absolutely certain way of bringing this nation to ruin, of preventing all possibility of its continuing to be a nation at all, would be to permit it to become a tangle of squabbling nationalities ….

Theodore Roosevelts
26th U.S. President
"Father" of Modern America

We do not have to visit a madhouse to find disordered minds;
our planet is the mental institution of the universe. [1815]

Johann Wolfgang Von Goethe
German Poet, Statesman, Scientist
1749 – 1832

His faculties refer to natures out of him, and predict the world he is to inhabit, as the fins of the fish foreshow that water exists, or the wings of an eagle in the egg presuppose air. Insulate him and you destroy him. He cannot live without a world. Put Napoleon in an island prison, let his faculties find no men to act on, no Alps to climb, no stake to play for, and he would beat the air and appear stupid.
[History] [1841]

Ralph Waldo Emerson
American Philosopher
1803 – 1882

Socialism itself can hope to exist only for brief periods here and there, and then only through the exercise of the extremest terrorism. For this reason it is secretly preparing itself for rule through fear and is driving the word 'justice' into the heads of the half-educated masses like a nail so as to rob them of their reason ... and to create in them a good conscience for the evil game they are to play. [Human, All Too Human, Aphorism 473] [1878]

… …

He who fights with monsters should be careful lest he thereby becomes a monster. And if thou gaze long into an abyss, the abyss will also gaze into thee. [Beyond Good and Evil, Aphorism 146] [1886]

Friedrich Nietzsche
German Philosopher
1844 – 1900

Education, which was at first made universal in order that all might be able to read and write, has been found capable of serving quite other purposes. By instilling nonsense it unifies populations and generates collective enthusiasm.

… …

Some "advanced thinkers" are of the opinion that anyone who differs from the conventional opinion must be in the right. This is a delusion; if it were not, truth would be easier to come by than it is. There are infinite possibilities of error, and more cranks take up unfashionable errors than unfashionable truths.

… …

… I asked him what it was, and he said it was the statement that Julius Caesar is dead. When I asked him why he did not agree, he drew himself up and said: "Because I am Julius Caesar." These examples show that you cannot make sure of being right by being eccentric.

… …

A wise man will enjoy the goods of which there is a plentiful supply, and of intellectual rubbish he will find an abundant diet, in our own age as in every other. [An Outline of Intellectual Rubbish] [1943]

Bertrand Russell
British Philosopher
1872 – 1970

But an effect can become a cause, reinforcing the original cause and producing the same effect in an intensified form, and so on indefinitely. A man may take to drink because he feels himself to be a failure, and then fail all the more completely because he drinks. It is rather the same thing that is happening to the English language. It becomes ugly and inaccurate because our thoughts are foolish, but the slovenliness of our language makes it easier for us to have foolish thoughts. The point is that the process is reversible.

… …

Two qualities are common to all of them. The first is staleness of imagery; the other is lack of precision. The writer either has a meaning and cannot express it, or he inadvertently says something else, or he is almost indifferent as to whether his words mean anything or not. This mixture of vagueness and sheer incompetence is the most marked characteristic of modern English prose, and especially of any kind of political writing. As soon as certain topics are raised, the concrete melts into the abstract and no one seems able to think of turns of speech that are not hackneyed: prose consists less and less of *words* chosen for the sake of their meaning, and more and more of *phrases* tacked together like the sections of a prefabricated hen-house.

… …

Let me give another example of the kind of writing that they lead to. This time it must of its nature be an imaginary one. I am going to translate a passage of good English into modern English of the worst sort. Here is a well-known verse from ***Ecclesiastes:***

> I returned and saw under the sun, that the race is not to the swift, nor the battle to thestrong, neither yet bread to the wise, nor yet riches to men of understanding, nor yet favour to men of skill; but time and chance happeneth to them all.

Here it is in modern English:

> Objective considerations of contemporary phenomena compel the conclusion thatsuccess or failure in competitive activities exhibits no tendency to be commensuratewith innate capacity, but that a considerable element of the unpredictable must

invariably be taken into account.

This is a parody, but not a very gross one. Exhibit (3) above, for instance, contains several patches of the same kind of English. It will be seen that I have not made a full translation. The beginning and ending of the sentence follow the original meaning fairly closely, but in the middle the concrete illustrations — race, battle, bread — dissolve into the vague phrases 'success or failure in competitive activities'. This had to be so, because no modern writer of the kind I am discussing — no one capable of using phrases like 'objective considerations of contemporary phenomena' — would ever tabulate his thoughts in that precise and detailed way. The whole tendency of modern prose is away from concreteness. Now analyze these two sentences a little more closely. The first contains forty-nine words but only sixty syllables, and all its words are those of everyday life. The second contains thirty-eight words of ninety syllables: eighteen of those words are from Latin roots, and one from Greek. The first sentence contains six vivid images, and only one phrase ('time and chance') that could be called vague. The second contains not a single fresh, arresting phrase, and in spite of its ninety syllables it gives only a shortened version of the meaning contained in the first. Yet without a doubt it is the second kind of sentence that is gaining ground in modern English. I do not want to exaggerate. This kind of writing is not yet universal, and outcrops of simplicity will occur here and there in the worst-written page. Still, if you or I were told to write a few lines on the uncertainty of human fortunes, we should probably come much nearer to my imaginary sentence than to the one from *Ecclesiastes.*

As I have tried to show, modern writing at its worst does not consist in picking out words for the sake of their meaning and inventing images in order to make the meaning clearer. It consists in gumming together long strips of words which have already been set in order by someone else, and making the results presentable by sheer humbug. The attraction of this way of writing is that it is easy. It is easier — even quicker, once you have the habit — to say *In my opinion it is not an unjustifiable assumption that* than to say *I think*. If you use ready-made phrases, you not only don't have to hunt about for the words; you also don't have to bother with the rhythms of your sentences since these phrases are generally so arranged as to be more or less euphonious.

...

He cannot say outright, 'I believe in killing off your opponents when you can get good results by doing so'. Probably, therefore, he will say something like this:

> "While freely conceding that the Soviet regime exhibits certain features which the humanitarian may be inclined to deplore, we must, I think, agree that a certain curtailment of the right to political opposition is an unavoidable concomitant of transitional periods, and that the rigors which the Russian people have been called upon to undergo have been amply justified in the sphere of concrete achievement."

The inflated style itself is a kind of euphemism. A mass of Latin words falls upon the facts like soft snow, blurring the outline and covering up all the details. The great enemy of clear language is insincerity. When there is a gap between one's real and one's declared aims, one turns as it were instinctively to long words and exhausted idioms, like a cuttlefish spurting out ink. In our age there is no such thing as "keeping out of politics." All issues are political issues, and politics itself is a mass of lies, evasions, folly, hatred, and schizophrenia. When the general atmosphere is bad, language must suffer. I should expect to find -- this is a guess which I have not sufficient knowledge to verify -- that the German, Russian and Italian languages have all deteriorated in the last ten or fifteen years, as a result of dictatorship.

I have not here been considering the literary use of language, but merely language as an instrument for expressing and not for concealing or preventing thought. Stuart Chase and others have come near to claiming that all abstract words are meaningless, and have used this as a pretext for advocating a kind of political quietism. Since you don't know what Fascism is, how can you struggle against Fascism? One need not swallow such absurdities as this, but one ought to recognize that the present political chaos is connected with the decay of language, and that one can probably bring about some improvement by starting at the verbal end. If you simplify your English, you are freed from the worst follies of orthodoxy. You cannot speak any of the necessary dialects, and when you make a stupid remark its stupidity will be obvious, even to yourself. Political language - and with variations this is true of all political parties, from Conservatives to Anarchists - is designed to make lies sound truthful and murder respectable, and to give an appearance of solidity to pure wind. [Politics and the English Language] [1946]

George Orwell
British Essayist, Novelist
1903 – 1950

Within the next generation I believe that the world's rulers will discover that infant conditioning and narco-hypnosis are more efficient, as instruments of government, than clubs and prisons, and that the lust for power can be just as completely satisfied by suggesting people into loving their servitude as by flogging and kicking them into obedience. In other words, I feel that the nightmare of *Nineteen Eighty-Four* is destined to modulate into the nightmare of a world having more resemblance to that which I imagined in *Brave New World*.
[Letter to Orwell] [1949]

Aldous Huxley
British Essayist, Novelist
1894 – 1963

Former President Gerald Ford, a 33rd degree Mason, wears a necktie with the "cross of Baphomet" emblem of the occultic OTO and British satanist Aleister Crowley. The symbol is also worn by the Sovereign Grand Commander of Scottish Rite Freemasonry. Ford was a member of the Warren Commission that came up with the preposterous conclusion that Lee Harvey Oswald acted alone in the assassination of President John F. Kennedy. Chief Justice Earl Warren, like Ford and all the other members of the Commission, was a 33rd degree Mason. [Codex Magica] [2005]

Texe Marrs
Journalist, Theologian
No relation to Jim
1944 -

Prior to the 1930s, paper bills could be redeemed for gold, since Section 10 of the Constitution specifies gold and silver as the only lawful tender. … Usury was once considered
a sin by the Christian churches and, until recently, usury - defined as excessively high interest - was a crime punishable by fine or jail.

Money today is increasingly mere electronic blips in a computer accessed by plastic cards at ATMs. There is nothing to back it up. Yet this illusory money is loaned at interest by great institutions. As the total amount of money grows, its worth decreases. This is called inflation,
in effect a built-in tax on the use of money. And inflation can be manipulated, upwards
or downwards, by those who control the flow of paper money, or these electronic blips.

Only two U.S. presidents have attempted to issue interest-free money: Abraham Lincoln, who printed "Greenbacks" to finance his war against the Southern Rebellion; and John F. Kennedy, who in 1963 issued "United States Notes" through the U.S. Treasury rather than "Federal Reserve Notes." It may not be sheer coincidence that both of these men were shot in the head in a public place. It has proven hazardous to one's health to thwart the international bankers. [Is the Federal Reserve a Scam?] [2008]

Jim Marrs
Journalist, Historian
No relation to Texe
1943 – 2017

First Champion for the Middle Class

damned new world order globalists … drank … ate

Tax Paying Middle Class's … Brains … Flesh … Blood

Thus Hinterlanders felt not one bit great

Yes, sweeter seemed God's brimstones … flames … plagues … floods

Then out of nowhere came The Donald Trump

Who vowed … to dumpster all that VD dreck

To drain the swamp, to haul to garbage dumps

To make these clowns … less known than Amalek …

Laws, policies, of bolshevik parades

All drug cartels, all nafta banksterviks

All arab terrorists who would invade

Would be imprisoned … next to Willie Slick:

The end: of fee-fie-foe-fummed-humptied chumps:

America: Great Once Again: By Trump … …

Queen Hillary Artillery

She's badly balled … and hanging chadly chained

To boring whoremonger … Her Bonehead Bill

The "smartest" woman ever … only gained

The classic "dumb blond" cred … lips roto-tilled …

She rode Bill's coded kale, coat tails, propped gropes

Well-calibrated cog, her red shield rigs

Venereal disease, small price for hope

This planet's power trip, she prepped to dig

Steamrolling global moles … the joy … the pride

Each week, her heart, mind, soul, she'd re-invent

All non-fake failures deemed, her funkifieds

But money grows on trees … to pay their rent:

Their commissars: still rape God's Universe:

They snap-swipe mattress … shoe box … wallet … purse … …

Bill, Barry, Big Foot Fairy Tales

Bizarre … how Bill and Barry stole the votes

Each one … crowned Emperor … not once … but twice

The odds of that occurring, you should note

Like Maui waters floating glaciered ice …

But never underestimate hell's hate

That pumps through globalists' satanic veins

Vast millions fear their children's empty plates

Small savaged savings spilling down the drain

Both Bill and Barry "loved" the Middle Class

Of Middle Class's taxes to be cut

Twin boneheads tweedled dumb as Horse's Ass

Each bum had belched … stiletto-ing our guts:

To save us all: each claimed in whores and words:

Yes, all of us … force fed … their piss … their turds … …

So Why Then Waste the Blood and Ink

Can lead the blind to Inner Soul of Christ, but cannot make them blink

Can lead the globalists to galaxies of gold, but cannot make them clink

Can lead the women on ross-franken-bills, but cannot make them fink

Can lead the women in the tarot cards, but cannot make them jinx

Can lead the people globalism's gate, but cannot make them lynx

Can lead the people communism's cart, but cannot make them mink

Can lead a man to vats of olive oil, but cannot make him shrink

Can lead a man to wormwood's end of days, but cannot make him stink

Can lead a man to wisdom's pearly gates, but cannot make him think

And you can lead a horse to Heaven's streams, but cannot make it drink

But if the horse's mouth won't even drink …

So why … then waste … the blood … and ink … …

Spring, 2018

The President's Tenacity

The President, both hounded and confounded by his enemies, lies vanquished --- dead --- from enemies and rivalries … indeed no dreams of victories or revelries:

Regarding other matters still more obvious: the sun's been rising in the west, and setting in the east; more blizzards have now blanketed the Sahara Desert and the Caribbean Islands, with 50 feet of snow; Federal Reserved, VD Deserved, International Gangsters Banksters Be Served, New World Order governments have released formerly Fort Knox guarded formulas, equations, calculations, and innovations, stolen by FBI Deep Staters (yes, they have been around damn near forever) from Serbian-Austrian scientist-inventor Nikola Tesla, upon his unexplained unexpected death in 1943 in New York City, where Tesla had discovered how ocean water can be desalinated, at mere nickel a barrel; and how car and truck engines can be assembled or retrofitted to run 1000 miles on a gallon of gasoline, at mere penny a gallon; Jennifer Lawrence, Katy Perry, Amy Schumer, Stormy Daniels, Material Madonna, Barbra Streisand, Jane Fonda, and Queen Hillary Artillery have all accepted lifetime memberships with the Catholic Little Sisters of the Poor; and have all taken, with right hand raised and left hand rested on The Good Book (KJV), vows of sanity, chastity, modesty, poverty, sobriety, and veracity, but especially sanity; Chuck Todd, Jimmy Kimmel, Alec Baldwin, Harvey Weinstein, Woody Allen, Keith Richard, Paul McCartney, Warren Beatty, Jack Nicholson, Peter Fonda, Bill Clinton Bonehead, Oh Bonehead, and Joe Bonehead, have all accepted lifetime human waste disposal positions in villages in jungles of Africa and South America; and have all taken, with right hand raised and left rested on The Good Book (KJV), vows of sanity, chastity, modesty, poverty, sobriety, and veracity, but especially sanity; the big dogs, (or mangy mutts), at ABC, CBS, NBC, Apple, Facebook, Google, Reuters, Yahoo; Disney (original founder Walt Disney must be vomiting in his grave); other Hollywood horse hockey heavyweights; CNN (see TBS), TBS (see HBO), HBO (see Time-Warner), Time-Warner (see Warner Media), Warner Media (see ATT), ATT (see Federal Reserve), Federal Reserve (see International Banksters), International Banksters (see New World Order), have started wearing full body cams 24/7 and also having revolving drones head/toe, including, but not limited to, urine, feces, kale, tofu, drugs, booze, orgies, and rock and roll, with all corporate policies and decisions written and printed in triplicate for global distribution and examination; Lynch, Holder, Comey, Sessions, Rosenstein, Wray, Mueller, Strzok, Price, Ohr, Steele, and their overlords the Bushes, the Clintons, and other New World Order Globalists, have resigned not only from public life but also from private life, dumpstered the 49 questions they had for President Trump, and resolved to answer, under oath, for Rush Limbaugh, Michael Savage, Sean Hannity, Tucker Carlson, Mark Levin, Texe Marrs, John Hagee, Franklin Graham, Doug Batchelor, Ann Coulter, Laura Ingraham, Michelle Malkin, Marjory Ross, Larry Elder, Thomas Sowell, and Walter Williams, the 490 questions each one of them had prepared for Mule Mueller and his merry band of Deep State Skulls and Bones; more accurately known as Numbskulls and Boneheads; NSA, CIA, DOJ, FBI, and all local keystone cops around the country have once again directed their attention towards the apprehension of rapists, rioters, murderers, and terrorists; and not towards the apprehension and incarceration of President Trump's supporters at peaceful rallies --- this historian has friends and family members who attended those peaceful rallies, who were beaten, almost to death, because they were breathing --- finally, Lenin, Stalin, Trotsky, Minh, Mao, and Castro all hollered up from their hangouts in hell that they found a snowball down there, around 100 circles below Dante's 9th one, that evidences excellent chances of remaining frozen forever; the Nation's welfare recipients signed contracts agreeing to reimburse the Nation's Great American Middle Class Taxpayers perpetually and retroactively; when not working 3 jobs to offset lifetimes of getting paid for getting laid, getting drunk, and getting stoned, liberal baby boomers, gen-x-ers, and millennials stowed suntan oil and surfboards and motored to the North Pole, the new surf city, catching waves, and sitting on top of the world.

This age is strange.

This age is deranged.

America is no longer land of the free, and home on the range, where skies are not cloudy all day. Fake entertainment empires, fake education empires, and fake news empires for decades have been doling out the land and its beauty and its bounty to invading armies from the other 4 ½ four continents. Instead of combat boots, these armies lace up high top Nikes; instead of metal helmets, they pull down vagina hats; instead of belts of bullets, they strap on strings of pearls and sapphires. That the members may not even know their possible deaths may prove to be irrelevant was and is, well, irrelevant. Silly assed sofa socialists like Pete Seeger or Peter, Paul, and Mary singing "this land is your land" and "this land is our land" have proven kindergarten cute and Sabbath white lace sweet. However, the idea that minimum wage bartenders in Motown, minimum wage hair dressers in Mobile, and minimum wage garbage truck drivers near the Mojave Desert, all of whom are struggling to make ends meet, owe invading armies anything at all after 100 years of global warfare to defeat dictators and global welfare to treat their victims, must be labeled just plain crazy. As to pie in the sky notions of "free," if, after a hard taxing week feeding children and parents and heeding bosses and bankers, he or she wishes to enjoy ribeye steak drowned in mushrooms, the anti-Steak and Baked Potato with Butter and Sour Cream Stormtroopers will find them and curse them until the hell, that anti-Steak Stormtroopers deny exists, freezes over. The skies have no blue, and they nearly have no sun, not because of cars and trucks and their pollution, but because the invading armies and their spies and allies and deep staters already here are burning down millions of acres of forests, which local politicians regret, but not enough to cease to permit. This time tested strategy of create a problem and then the solution guarantees millions of votes offered to Democrats, and millions more in disaster relief tax dollars pilfered from President Trump.

In this age, there are few true scientists, social or physical. At your local dive or drive through or coffee house or bar and grill, it would prove faster and smarter and easier to locate and interview a bigfoot from America's far northern frozen tundra or an alien from across the far corners of God's Cosmos. Blaming President Trump for every ridiculously and repetitively wrong climate change implied forecast, even local television weather gals audition for Queen Hillary Artillery supporting roles, staring into the cameras, cross-eyed, knock-kneed, silicone-boobed, booze-and-cannabis-and-bubble-gum-brained. Nikola Tesla once said that "The scientists of today think deeply instead of clearly; one must be sane to think clearly, but one can think deeply and be quite insane." The same could be said of almost all the Poison Ivy Leagues and all the Poachered Ivory Towers indoctrinated imbeciles that inhabit that vast, limitless, mad maximus, intellectual wasteland, known euphemistically as the self-decreed and self-crowned artistic-political left. President Trump still stands --- strong, erect, elusive, and resourceful. His victories and revelries grate at his haters even more than his haters, like hounds from hell, charge to rip, growl, and devour a perfectly fire pit roasted longhorn steer. The indestructible fact is that the President continues both to battle and to triumph --- with integrity, ingenuity, and indestructible tenacity.

Summer, 2018

In Garbage Dumps by Mister Trump

Part I – So Enter Donald Trump

After 18 months into his Presidency, our President Trump has triumphantly triple jumped his way not only into the history books but also into the hearts and souls of the members of the Great American Middle Class who supported him, voted for him, and remain loyal to him, both defiantly and deafeningly. But even as late as the summer of 2015, the fake media empires, the smart money, the beautiful people, and the members of that vast, limitless, mad maximus, intellectual wasteland, known euphemistically as the self-decreed and self-crowned artistic-political left, all stated confidently and new world orderly that Trump was an overlord, an underdog, and, therefore, an afterthought. Most of them didn't know him, most who knew him didn't like him, and most who didn't like him hated him. He had his lovely wife and family and TV show and billions, and he globetrotted and hard-hatted and hard-headed and laid the foundations and built the reputation for world class hotels and lost paradise resorts. More qualifying would have been background in community activism, poison ivy league shysterism, peanut butter spines, and steer manure brains.

Both globalist socialist John McCain, definitive Republican in Name Only (RINO) who crashed in 2008, and globalist socialist Mitt Romney, yet another RINO, who crashed in 2012, both announced they would not run again. In his Navy days, John "Crash Cup" McCain crashed 5 Navy planes, one into the U.S.S. Forrestal in 1967 that killed over 100 Navy personnel. This final symbolic New World Order deep state destruction of deeply fear filled James Forrestal could not be more devious. The warning to generals, admirals, citizens, and generations could not be more obvious. Gallows rumor still circulates that Crash Cup had his name cleared and revered cleanly and conveniently through rewritten and re-computed Navy records, by cross-eyed, lame-brained, boot-licking, Numb Skulls and Bone Heads bred USMC Captain, named Robert "Mule" Mueller III. Yes, THAT John McCain. And, yes, THAT

Robert "Mule" Mueller III. In the late 1950s and early 1960s, Mitt "Pit Stop-Belly Flop" Romney's father, George "Junkyard" Romney, drove first, as CEO, a car company straight into the ground, then drove second, as governor, the state of Michigan straight into the ground. Junkyard George in the early 1960s was the definitive liberal Rockefeller Republican Moron who planted, watered, and fertilized the seeds that stinkweeded into the present day rotting catastrophe called Detroit. Back in 1963-1964, all the polls and all the experts said he could have beaten Goldwater for the Republican nomination and then beaten Democrat LBJ for the Presidency. To this very day, young Pit Stop-Belly Flop worships his father Junkyard George. Mitt's running for President, forever, has always been his guarding and honoring and his father, forever. Most Americans and most other global citizens do not know most WWII babies and most Baby Boomers are buried still believing it is 1968, still protesting the Vietnam War, and still campaigning for Eugene McCarthy or Robert Kennedy. Worse, to this very day, young Pit Stop-Belly Flop does not offer any apologies for his fumbling father's fundamental failures. He does not even offer any lessons learned. All he has offered to millions who voted for him and supported him are sickening silence on Emperor Bill Bonehead (former President Bill Clinton, Jan 1993 – Jan 2001), even more sickening silence on Emperor Oh Bonehead (former President Barack Obama, Jan 2009 – Jan 2017), and hell sent banshee-like screaming sessions at President Trump. But, during the 8 years of Bill Bonehead and 8 more of Oh Bonehead, where they or their cronies and flunkies venereal diseased the White House as if it were a whore house, young Pit Stop-Belly Flop never said one damn word.

Sunday driving RINOs Junkyard George, Crash Cup, and Pit Stop - Belly Flop, three blind-deaf-and-dumb mice, yes dumb as in dumb, Tweedledee, Tweedledum, and Tweedledumber, three New World Order liberal Rockefeller Republicans, never won the White House. Thank God. If so, each would have crashed Air Force One to the bottom of Lake Superior, next to the SS Edmund Fitzgerald, where in 1975 fake news empires presented total absence of regret and sadness after full crew had perished in the iron ore filled, coal fired freighter's sinking. Yes, the deep state and the fake media empires have been around a damn long time. And their hatred for oil and gas and coal and the industrial heartland of America, the resurrecting hinterland of the planet, has been around for a damn long time. They have proven it time and time and time again. The most recent time occurred in 2016 when Queen Hillary Artillery thought it was hilarious to tell a group of West Virginia coal miners that it would be hilarious when she as President would shut down the Nation's coal mines and how it would be equally hilarious when she destroyed all the coal jobs of all the folks at whom she was laughing her fat, ugly, rumpled butt off.

On the other hand, Donald Trump entered the race simply promising, among other things, not only to never repeat these past, present, and future fears, flaws, and fundamental failures; but also, and more importantly, to make the country great again, meaning, more specifically, the members of America's 100-year forgotten, 100- year downtrodden, 100-year sinking to the bottom, Tax Paying Middle Class respected. Again.

Part II – Thus Exit No Dice RINO Mice

For 2016, a record high 17 Republicans stepped into the ring for the right to win the White House. All the Republicans, except one, presented themselves as standard operating procedure types and basic beltway establishment types and as such for months had been dully and steadily plodding along. They all made snails look like Olympic sprinters. The craziest thing is that each one of them presented himself or herself and policies and positions as new or special or historically unique. Pundits and pollsters on left and right ranked these pretenders and contenders, where time would tell which, lowest to highest: Jim Gilmore, Bobby Jindal, George Pataki, Rick Santorum, Scott Walker, Mike Huckabee, Chris Christie, Carly Fiorina, Rick Perry, Lindsay Graham, Ben Carson, John Kasich, Marco Rubio, Rand Paul, Ted Cruz, and Jeb Bush.

Jeb Bush, according to all fake media empires left and right and in between, reigned as New World Order's # 1 heavyweight. He was the son of a former President (Old Bush, Jan 1989 – Jan 1993). His father used the words "New World Order" more often than current

Dummycrats use the words "collusion and impeachment." He was also the brother of a former President (Kid Bush, Jan 2001 – Jan 2009). His brother used the one trick pony phony, folksy, dopey, southern gentleman routine almost as often as another former President (Jimmy Carter, Jan 1977 – Jan 1980), more accurately known as Peanut Butter Brain. In true bipartisan fashion, both men produced the same destructive results, both economically here at home and militarily in the Middle East. After overspending by billions, Peanut Butter Brain could not find a few functional military helicopters to rescue American hostages from Iran. Two decades later, after overspending by billions, Kid Bush could not find a few desert terrain experts to find weapons of mass destruction in Iraq. Naturally, in the nutty world of modern politics, with all this family Presidential "success" behind him, Jeb the joker, lead clown in the Republican clown car, proved the highest qualification was yet another conservative who had conserved almost everything, except conservatism. Jalopy Jeb, former governor of diverse, cosmopolitan Florida, husband of and father through an educated attractive Hispanic wife, and adamant advocate of full amnesty and full citizenship for all illegal aliens from around the globe, was declared "the man." Fake media empires declared the Republican nomination was his to lose. Fake news empires concluded bottom line for Trump was he could not run. There was no way this side of Jack Dempsey and Rocky Marciano that Donald Trump could stand toe to toe in the ring with Jeb Bush, absorbing jab after jab. He could pretend a few billion dollars, bellow a few bombastic speeches, and butcher a few basics of grammar. But if he were dumb enough to run, the fake news empires had already laid the foundations to ensure that no voters would ever know him. If voters ever did know him, they would never vote for him. Like love and hate, arrogance is never constrained by time or space or heart or place or creed or race. The Messiah in Matthew 7 provided definitions, on which foundations were built on sand, and which foundations were built on rock, and which would last. Back then Roman Emperors paid a quarter penny's worth of attention to a "rabble rouser's" Laws and Truths and Principles and Commandments, and 2,000 years later actual and potential Presidential Emperors paid barely a quarter penny more, including inflation.

Those same fake news empires, that same smart money, those same beautiful people, and those same members of that vast, limitless, mad maximus, intellectual wasteland, known as the self-decreed and self-crowned artistic-political left, again declared confidently, again new world orderly, that, if U.S. N.Y.C. Citizen Trump did run in the Republican Presidential Primary, Candidate Trump would be not only be beaten, but also beaten badly. In the debates particularly, he would be exposed as a cauliflower-eared bum who knew nothing about defending the morals, customs, and traditions of our Judeo-Christian heritage, who knew nothing about the foundations of our Constitution, who knew nothing about the issues facing our Nation, and who knew nothing about the horrendous hardships methodically demolishing our Great American Middle Class. His own blood and his own tears would spill and flow all over his full thick blond-orange hair and his middle class double cheese burger body and over every square inch of every ring. Trump would never meet, let alone exceed, the abilities and qualifications of his rivals. He would be defeated easily and efficiently by Gilmore's military zeal, Jindal's Cajun craftiness, Pataki's planned patience, Santorum's decorum, Walker's minister's stance, Huckabee's Fox News pedigree, Christie's consistency, Fiorina's HP HD speed, Kasich's Reagan's 80s crutch, Perry's oil wildcatter's knack, Graham's grits and ham, Carson's surgeon's skill and care, Rubio's Cubano get up and go, Paul's libertarian's thrall, Cruz's Constitutional oozings, and Jeb Bush's father- and brother-trained dive bombing ambushes. Trump as the saying goes would be totally exposed as an amateur among professionals, pretender among contenders, and babe among behemoths. The idea that a zany, lucky, loudmouth zillionaire could relate to the average working stiff was ridiculous. Trump entered the race for the Republican nomination on June 16, 2015. After he did, every month on average one or two professional pretending behemoths had the ringside prize-fighting bell tolled for them. For those who have just emerged from a coma or just arrived from the Planet Uranus, the counter-punching Trump was not one of them.

By the end of the week of Christ's Birthday in 2015, Perry, Walker, Jindal, Graham, and Pataki had thrown in the towel, due to lack of mood, money, message, method, plasma, charisma, or combination thereof. They had spent a combined $70M or so for 8,000 popular votes and zero bound delegates. When Pataki quit few knew he had ever started. For Perry, Jindal, and Graham, it was mostly too little, too late, too plain, or too past. Brown bag lunch Perry from Texas could never brand a public hide. When Perry tossed around phrases like "vulture capitalists," support rolled away like tumbleweeds by dry dusty winds. Jindal with India heritage born in Baton Rouge Cajun country and educated at Brown in Ivy League, tried to take some of Paul's libertarian support, but that failed, so he fought for "free" trade that had always been global welfare and never free, at least not free for Middle Class Americans. Fox News would have him on once a week to blast Trump and brag $500M trade deficits, with China, Japan, Europe, Canada, and Mexico, as the Promised Land. Graham the gifted and ongoing gofer and grifter for Crash Cup McCain, tried to grab moderate positions as Crash Cup had in 2008, but went hard left with full amnesty and full citizenship for all illegal aliens. Everyone except Graham's South Carolina conservative supporters understood what a turncoat he had become. The most surprising early exit might have been Walker's. Boy Wonder son of a Baptist Minister from Delavan, WI, he had served as Governor of Wisconsin. He had fought 3 recall petitions, successfully; overcame powerful Democrat machine in Milwaukee, successfully; and drained the political swamp in state capital Marxist Madison, successfully. Walker's biggest problem was not his sober personality. His problem was that he refused to get cute, take loot, and sacrilegiously salute the globalist socialists, their artistic-political left, and their fake news empires. Pence has served well as VP, but Trump and Walker would have been truly a Dynamic Duo. House Speaker Paul Ryan, also from Wisconsin, has delightfully done all the things Walker would not. Ryan, aka Boy Blunder, who in 2012 choked and smoked with Pit Stop Belly Flop, aka Flatman Splatman, became the reigning Dynamic Dunderheads. A more dimwitted and New World Order puppet mastered pair could not be found on the planet. It is not a coincidence, in the House, Speaker Boy Blunder's revolving door exit has become, in the Senate, Flatman Splatman's revolving door entrance, who for all practical purposes in the Senate has replaced Crash Cup.

By the end of the week of Christ's Crucifixion and Resurrection in 2016, Gilmore, Christie, Santorum, Huckabee, Paul, Fiorina, Carson, and Rubio also had the ringside bell tolled for them, all for the same reasons as the first five, plus a few more. They had spent a combined $280M or so for 4,624,152 popular votes and 132 bound delegates, 123 of which went to Rubio. Like Pataki, Gilmore quit before anyone knew he had started. Moderate New Jersey Governor Christie had advantages over McCain and Romney. With booming voice and east coast big state presence, he drew law and order support from his days as U.S. Attorney for New Jersey. But multiple scandals and grubby glad-handing with Emperor Oh Bonehead ended his chances. Social conservative Santorum went exactly as far as he did in 2012, namely, nowhere. He was out of money and out of ideas. His main themes of anti-abortion and pro-prayer were commendable, but came with sincerity questionable due to weird women. Those themes alone would not, because they could not, carry him to the White House. Moreover, candidates had been pushing those two themes since Reagan ran against incumbent Ford in 1976. However, abortion was still the law of the land, and the law of the jungle was still the law in the high schools, colleges, and universities. Huckabee had more of each than Santorum, and more commitment to the same two main themes, with more polish thanks to his Fox News analyst role. But the results were the same. Abortion and prayer had taken back seats to out of control border crossings and out of control terrorist bombings. Both Paul and Fiorina hit the economic themes hard, but the ridiculously wrong ones, i.e., NAFTA so nifty and China so thrifty.

Early on, with Hollywoodly hidden, illegally weighted gloves, Rubio landed a few punches, and thus won the 4th most votes and delegates. But, later on, when exposed, showing no loins and no clothes, Rubio groped and folded like Sheryl Crowed toilet paper. The raw and rambling and repulsive Rubio lost so much support so fast so far, he pulled a page from the globalist socialist playbooks of Bill Bonehead and Oh Bonehead and dove headlong into the waterless concrete pool of the politics of personal destruction. He lobbed jabbering stabs with the hand-size-loin-size myth, staggering and proving the reality, aka Jimmy Peanut Butter Brain, of peanut-sized hands, peanut-sized loins, and, worst of all, peanut-sized brains. Candidate Trump almost doubling the vote pounded Rubio into the sands of the beaches of Rubio's home state of Florida. It ended there, for Rubio; one, two, three; grim-snotted, rim-shotted, tequila-sotted. O Rubio, O Rubio, wherefore barf thou, O Rubio. In Shakespearean twist, he did not deny his name but he did deny his Republican Conservative political father Ronald Reagan. Rubio crawled off the canvas and into the casket. All the Juliets did not, and searching for other star-crossed lovers the gals returned to surfing the oceans and the net. In the end the Cubano modern combo of Romeo and Cicero imploded into a modern combo of Groucho, Chico, and Harpo.

John "Krash Kup" Kasich lost almost as much ground almost as fast as Rubio, but kept running, crunching, and rum dumming, into the ring posts, when not into the sledgehammer-like gloved fists of Candidate Trump. Krash Kup, like his Republican In Name Only (RINO) idols Crash Cup, Flatman-Splatman, and Boy Blunder, strapped on his ultra-teensy-weensy Reagan Republican jock strap just long enough to prance prettily and pristinely around the ring. He ran around and roared that he alone carried the torch for former President Reagan, Jan 1981 – Jan 1989, and that he and the Gipper were joined at the hip. Kasich was hipper and was sired by the big dipper and wore the ruby slippers to take one and all back to the Wizard of Oz. He joined Reagan in school boy dreams or in practical politics through fax machines and paper clips. Reagan entered the Oval Office in 1981; whereas Kasich the House of Representatives in 1983. Reagan entered office and promised to end Ford-Nixon-Rockefeller high taxes, inflation, deficits, and Communist Russia; whereas Kasich entered with a loose love of Nixon's détente, lumpy libertarianism, and plenty of pictures of his college days meeting with then President Nixon, Jan 1969 – Aug 1974. Drafted to serve on the House Armed Services Committee, Kasich seemed determined to take the Department of Defense, already cut off at the knees by Presidents Ford and Carter, and to meat ax still more, to the hips. The fact is that he worked too closely and too cozily and too soap operatically with a certain fellow House member, African-American Ron Dellums, of Oakland, CA. The dangerous Black Panthers praising Dellums was coolly articulate, articulately cruel, super fly suited, and GQ recruited. The dude spent almost 3 decades in the House as an admitted and devoted white hating Black nationalist-socialist. Dellums had the ultra-klutzy Kasich, amongst other places, in his hip pocket. Somehow it is never threatening nor hypocritical when millions strut intimidatingly in battle fatigues.

Perhaps this is what in 2016 Kasich meant by "hip." But, for all the endless talk, Reagan and Kasich never did end endless debt; they never did end bloated budgets; they never did end Middle Class destroying taxes. Kasich never mentioned these damning facts. Later in the 90s as member and later Chairman of the House Budget Committee, he gleefully guided President New World Order Old Bush's Great American Middle Class tax increase --- the conservatism killing read the lips kind --- through the House and Senate and onto Old Bush's desk for signature. Then with Old Bush and Cheney and all the other nameless shameless globalist socialist charlatans, Kasich gleefully gutted the Nation's weapons systems and entire defense industry. Kasich was instrumental in establishing the Base Re-Alignment and Closure Commission (BRAC). The stated purpose was to streamline military bases; the actual purpose was to castrate our Nation's military forces. Decades later the Communist Chinese took full advantage in economics and the Muslim Arabs took full advantage as terrorists. This "Peace Dividend" was supposed to balance the Federal budget and pay off most of the National debt. But of course endless debt and unbalanced budgets only went from bad to worse. Peace dividend mutated into more global war end. In the late 90s Kasich finally helped to balance the budget. But this was due almost exclusively to the superhuman efforts of House Speaker Newt Gingrich and his Contract with America in engineering a Republican majority for 1995, for the first time in half a century. Kasich was kindly allowed to claim the titles of head bonehead and chief bean counter. He did join Queen Hillary and Bill Bonehead on the Hillary care brigade. By then most party pros knew the prognosis was power crazed little crackpot that needed a frontal lobotomy. He bounced over to bankrupted Lehman Brothers, corrupted Fox News, and disrupted Ohio's Governorship. All this bouncing around banged his bonehead brain with the same effect as a lobotomy. Or perhaps he thought not hips but lips since Reagan enjoyed jelly beans. A dozen times cameras caught Kasich salivating over and devouring ribs and fried chicken and corn on the cob. He seemed to have been not only born in a barn but also raised with the pigs. With full mouth already mouthing off for 2020, clinging to and clamoring over the past slumped the sloppy slightly mad political Clem Kadiddlehopper.

Senator Ted Cruz of Texas stampeded like a focused and ferocious longhorn into the ring and went toe to toe with International Man for All Seasons and International Plan for All Reasons, aka TKO Master Donald J. Trump. Most athletes in general and most prizefighters in particular exhibited either speed or power. Very few were born with both. In the world of heavyweight boxing, the only one blessed with both was Cassius Clay, who could float like a butterfly and sting like a bee. Muhammed Ali due to Islam and napalms and cherry bombs soon floated like a beached whale and stood like a termite-ridden tree. It is almost impossible to be supreme both athletically and politically. Just ask Colin Kaepernick and all the other kneeling and knock-kneed knot heads and knuckleheads. In the world of heavyweight politics, the only one blessed with both was, and still is, Donald J. Trump. Ted Cruz, the other Republicans, the other Conservatives, Queen Hillary Artillery, Bill Bonehead, Oh Bonehead, and the fake media empires still haven't figured that out. Yes, Cruz could throw a punch. He landed some on Trump that could have knocked down Trump's NYC Tower. But for every punch Cruz threw, the perfectly poised, perfectly patient, perfectly protracted, perfectly professional, and perfectly counter-punching, calculating, calibrating Trump, in return, planted 3 or 4 or 5 planet rattlers, that sometimes knocked the planet off its axis, and that always knocked the horns off Cruz and into the bottom of Rio Grande River. Yes, Cruz presented respected positions on issues both clearly and cleanly. He ran as and became known as a Constitutional Conservative and a Principled Constitutionalist. Cruz was and is a smart man and even smarter politician. However, like all others before him whom Trump had defeated, Cruz had become too enamored with Nixon-Ford-Reagan-Old Bush-Kid Bush beltway mentalities and too alienated from the Hinterland's Main Street and Wagon Train Realities. For the few remaining Reagan Ronaldus Magnus fans still out there, what kind of "Principled Conservative" allows New World Order Old Bush to ride shotgun as sidekick Jingles to Reagan's Wild Bill Hickok. Politicians south of the Mason-Dixon Line, and especially Texans like Cruz, normally did not make this sort of fatal boot hill express mistake. Even when inside the beltway for months at time, at a time when there were no cell phones, no computers, and no 24/7 Fox/CNN, men like Lyndon Johnson and John Connally always had one had on the throats of their political opponents in DC, and the other hand on the pulse of their constituents back home in Texas. Cruz, although he seems to have learned this lesson for his 2024 Republican Presidential run, did not learn it time to change Trump's victory in 2016.

Neither Cruz nor the others grasped the fact that interpretations of the Constitution since the early 1960s had become almost idiotically inaccurate. Idiotic inaccuracy had been exceeded only by cart before the horse idolatry and irrelevancy. Like all the others, Cruz could neither see nor smell the global dung hill being dumped on the Great American Middle Class. Abortion on demand was bad but worse was decades of design of taxes, spending, and exploding national debt methodically murdering Middle Class families. Annual trade deficits of $500 billion or more with Canada, Mexico, Asia, Europe, and Arab Nations, followed by annual $500 billion or more in weapons system for all the global warfare and global welfare, were not Constitutional. They were Catastrophic. There was nothing Principled or Constitutional in the Cruz slogan of "Principled Constitutionalism." Powerful conservatives had no idea that their relentlessly ridiculous promotion for a half century of outsourcing of American jobs, profits, pensions, and industries had made "conservatism" as modern and relevant as Ford's old Model T, if not the primitive caveman's club. Trump since the day he started running pounded and pounded and pounded that message home 365/24/7 until he was elected President. Like all the others, Cruz was almost biologically clueless and genetically deaf when average Americans demanded immigration policies that allow criminal aliens to enter the country illegally, collect welfare, and be allowed citizenship, should be terminated immediately. Cruz and all the others in the 2016 Republican clown car had both miscalculated the cultural landscape and underestimated a candidate --- Donald Trump --- to a degree never before seen in American history. It was similar to stating the Titanic could never sink. Reagan's "Revolution" was playground sandbox to what Trump was presenting. That Cruz and the others seemed stunned by Trump's demand for a border wall, and even more stunned by Americans across the political spectrum demanding it, seemed, well, stunning. Only those born, bred, or residing inside the beltway could think all this nonsense somehow constituted the Founding Fathers' thinking --- or God's Blessings.

Part III – Warped Bush World Wrecked and Wiped Away

Perhaps the only thing stranger than the strange tales of Carroll and Stevenson was the real life oh so strange case of Dr. Jebberwacky and Mr. Hide, aka Jeb Bush. Before 2016, pros and voters and pundits and leaders and dictators around the globe for years had been asking why John Ellis "Jeb" Bush was hiding, and not running for the highest and most powerful office in the free world, that had been destined to be his since the day he was born. After 2016, for centuries they would ask themselves why he had not remained hidden. Latest gallows humor started circulating that he had gone back home to Florida to hide with the gators in the swamps. Jebberwacky the swampy probably wished to ensure that, when it came time for President Trump to drain the last spoonful of swamp water, the tarnished silver spooned Jebberwacky could maintain the new leftwing addiction of drunken wonkiness or monkish drunkenness, or, simply, the thunderous Trump knockout blow of "low energy," that knocked Jebberwacky and the New World Order useless and senseless and into the middle of the next decade. But how could he have bottom fed and swamp bottomed to such a miserable and incomprehensible mess? Jebberwacky was the great-great-grandson of James Smith Bush, who during the Civil War era preached fiery sermons as a prominent Episcopal Minister in New Jersey and New England states. Jebberwacky was the great-grandson of Samuel Prescott Bush, who in early 1900s ran from the wrong side of the tracks to run railroad empires and industries and lock-stepped with the original Harrimans and Rockefellers on a first name basis; then served President Woodrow Wilson in WWI as liaison to defense industries; then through banking ties to Bernard Baruch helped sire the Federal Reserve System and grade the road for the New World Order.

Jebberwacky was the grandson of Prescott Sheldon Bush (Shell Game Sheldon), who roared, behind the scenes, as royally and recklessly as anyone during the roaring 1920s, having graduated from Yale with a stale diploma in potent elitism and arrogant aroma of millions made in Chinese Opium Trade and medallions earned from Skull and Bones Society, aka Numb Skull and Bone Heads Society. Banker Bush and pals functioned as power brokers and bank rollers to Deeply Devious,

Deeply Dangerous, and Deeply Destructive Deep State. Yes, they are that old, and that deep, and that dark. Perpetually shell gaming Sheldon married Dorothy Walker, daughter of his banker boss, one George Herbert Walker, who as primary member in Harriman's private banking empire poured millions of Opium dollars into the American economy, and bankrolled Bolsheviks in Russia and Nazis in Germany. He role played U.S. Senator from Connecticut in the 50s and supported martini slurping pal and extremely liberal Republican Nelson Rockefeller's Presidential plans in early 1960s. In true deep state Dr. Jebberwacky and Mr. Hide form: Sheldon did not support Goldwater; he did not support Reagan; however, he did support his pal Nelson; in 1976 his son and future President George HW supported Ford over Reagan; in 1976, 33rd degree freemason Goldwater supported 33rd degree freemason Ford over Reagan; in 1980, 33rd degree freemason Goldwater supported Numb Skull and Boneheaded George HW over Reagan; which explained clearly the true deep state motives and intentions of "Principled Conservative" Goldwater; finally, to bring the dark web both fully circled and fully clerical, in 1976, Reagan, often stating 11th commandment was that a Republican shall not criticize another Republican, not only ran against incumbent Republican President Gerald Ford, but also picked as his running mate Republican Senator Lowell Weicker, one of the most ridiculously leftwing fools in the Senate, and one of the first ones sitting on the Watergate Committee to call for President Richard Nixon's resignation. Shell game Sheldon's banking empire ensured CBS was the first and most extensive and most communist cuddling television network in America and ensured it stayed that way for decades. That move purchased Sheldon a seat on the CBS Board of Directors. Later as U.S. Senator, he championed President Dwight Eisenhower's and New York Governor Nelson Rockefeller's, and CBS's, nonsense that the Nation could not afford to provide middle class tax cuts or to investigate communists at the State Department. Except for minor on air spat between Dan Blather and GHW Bush aka NWO Bush in 1988, hardcore hard left no-holds-barred CBS founder William Paley's founding decree to current and future CBS comrades that they were barred from burning the Bushes had been obeyed.

Jebberwacky was the son of George Herbert Walker Bush (Floppy Sloppy Poppy) (Ronald Reagan's VP, Jan 1981 – Jan 1989) (President Jan 1989 – Jan 1993). Old Floppy Sloppy Poppy Bush was named for his maternal grandfather, George Herbert Walker. Growing up in New England during roaring 20s and Great Depression, at a time when New England still ruled the Nation culturally and politically, Poppy played and laughed like that infinitely small lucky handful of those who are almost never greatly depressed, and who are almost always depressingly great. America's Great Depression was concocted by GHW's grandfathers, father, and their international banker-global industrialist cronies and comrades. That Great Depression was strategically (strategery?) executed through one of their private standard business subsidiaries, also known as the Federal Reserve Banking System. Both then, and now, very few Americans were or are aware of the frightening fact that "the Fed" is a private institution, owned by private firms and private individuals, who, through 24, 7, 365, and 366 leap year global monetary manipulations, dictate to the Federal Government, all state and local Governments, and, most importantly, all Americans what they shall and shall not do. Competition is a hoax. Monopoly is a fact. After the turn of the prior century, after a series of preliminary meetings, that demon-seeded, witch's brewed leviathan, aka the Fed, came into existence 1909 – 1913 spanning (spawning?) both "hard right" Taft and "hard left" Wilson. It happened at Georgia's Jekyll Island. Hmm. Jekyll. Hyde. Jokers. Hide. Clearly one of those satanic clowns owned a devilishly clever sense of gallows humor. These facts are never mentioned by the fake news empires, and they are also never mentioned by the fake education empires, because their members are whoring around in brothels and cathouses with the members of the fake banking empires. Christened Episcopalian popular George to evoke images of slayers of dragons, slayers of serpents, and slayers of monsters, or perhaps slayers of U.S. Middle Class Taxpayers, the happy and popular Poppy edited school newspapers at Philips Academy, piloted Navy fighters during WWII, captained his Yale baseball team, and graduated Summa Cum Laude in Skull and Bones Society, with a PhD in Boneheaded Skullduggery.

Poppy the dad and granddad is now 94 and there have been in those 94 years at least 94 reasons for his having obtained the nickname Poppy. The important point here is that none of them are within 94 million light years of being true. Since entering the public eye, in the early 70s as President Nixon's Ambassador to the United Nations, then GOP Chairman, then to China, then as CIA Chief Spook overseeing the MK Ultra Program (yes, before, during, and after reign of Poppy, CIA "Technical Services Division" kept spiking punch bowls with LSD), many reasons have been given: calling his granddads Pop-Pop; calling his own dad Pop-Pop; both hopping and hoping to be like them; shooting pop guns; singing pop goes the weasel; munching popcorn, licking popsicles; popping young women's cherries while in the Navy, catching pop flies as the Yale varsity first baseman; popping young women's cherries while skulling and boning at Yale; building poppet valves while in the oil business in Texas; pulling pop tops off cans of cold brew at the end of the day; toasting pop tarts for his grandchildren when as CIA Chief Spook he was not toasting foreign spies; planting poplars on his estates when as CIA Chief Spook he was not planting foreign spies; promoting the old 19th century Populist Party, especially the positions of government ownership of railroads and a steep graduated income tax; popping off to the press in the 1980 Republican Presidential primary debates about Reagan's anger, because Reagan was understandably riled when his microphone was shut off, for which he had paid big money; popularizing the idea that if remotely connected to the left what is government's is government's, and what is the Middle Class Taxpaying Citizens is also government's; pretending to expose liberal poppycock while pretending to be a conservative Vice President; pretending to expose liberal poppycock while pretending to be a conservative President; popping into the American center and cultural mainstream, the term "New World Order" around 94,000 times in 4 years, while concealing his and his New World Order socialist globalists' true intentions.

Poppy was nicknamed for the Opium poppy. The Opium poppy is that Middle East and Far East plant that produces a white sticky semen-like substance that is extracted and processed into morphine, heroin, and other opioids. They are all hideously addictive and horrendously destructive. The Opium poppy has been growing on the planet and mutating normal intelligent men into morons and misfits and malcontents and murderers since Adam and Eve strolled in the Garden of Eden and Cain slaughtered his brother Abel. Were it not for the Divine and direct inspiration by and intervention of God, then ripeness of the Opium poppy would explain Moses' description of God's manufacturing Eve from Adam's ribs, and then a serpent's conversing with both of them in a garden, where bears and lions nibbled lettuce and blackberries, not sheep and goats. Except for the 12 tribes of Israel, all ancient tribes, cultures, peoples, and empires in Southern Europe, Eastern Europe, Middle East, and Far East in their symbols, drawings, carvings, and writings, mention opium, including the Egyptians, and before them the Sumerians, whose culture predated ancient Israelites by at least 1,000 years. The Opium poppy is never specifically mentioned in the Bible. However, there are references to wine of course but also, and more importantly, to "other strong drink," the latter of which evidences no consensus culturally or religiously. With thousands of years of opium poppy addiction now behind us, it is extremely clear why God would instruct Moses to call it "the forbidden fruit." Much more could be learned but most ancient writings by Jewish and Christian leaders and believers have been burned or destroyed by enemy empires, or discovered and secreted away by New World Order globalists and their governments. Did you really think that one of the last scenes in the first Steven Spielberg-George Lucas *Indiana Jones* movie, where Biblical Ark of the Covenant is nailed in a wooden crate stored away with millions of others in a warehouse, an accident? Just another Hollywood prank? Well, then, I have tropical swamplands at the North Pole I would like to sell you. That scene was New World Order globalists telling their cohorts that all in the world was, well, in perfect order. Only God Himself knows what other documents are hidden away in other caves besides Qumran's, in the mansions of the Bilderbergers, in underground facilities at Bohemian Grove, and in the dungeons of the Vatican, right next to Inquisition torture chambers. Only recently have we learned that during the British-Chinese Opium Trade of the 19th century, which the British imposed to cure their empire's terrible trade deficit, a handful of American families made Godless fortunes that only Judas Iscariot could fully appreciate. One of them was the Delanos, whose seed would be FDR; a second was the Forbes, whose seed would be John Kerry; a third was the Russell family, whose seed would found and fund the Yale University Skull and Bones Society (Numb Skulls and Bone Heads). Though back then technically legal, this Opium economic activity, this one truly polluting global monstrosity, was demonically unethical, especially for a Nation founded on the Biblical principles of New England Protestantism. Had they known, temperance groups would have stoned those hypocrites to death. Just like the Corleones in Coppola's *Godfather* soap operas, ways and means were needed to push all those hundreds of millions of Opium-laden dollars into the economy. Since they too made their fair share, fake media empires have been sickeningly silent.

Poppy was formally named for his maternal grandfather, George Herbert Walker. A descendent of Maryland slave owners and the son of an import-export businessman, Walker shrewdly shot into international banking, showered tokens on Yale Bonesmen, and later became President of Harriman and Brown Brothers, a well-heeled, and iron-heeled, private investment banking institution. It became one of the oldest and largest private ones in the world. Since his first day the goal of Walker and others was to keep Uncle Sam's hands off those Opium-laden dollars, and to keep Citizen Sam's mind on anything and everything else, such as the panic of 1907, with "solution" called the Federal Reserve, World War I, and leagues of nations. Walker's daughter Dorothy married Prescott Sheldon Bush, with Walker's blessing. With shell game Sheldon in the fold millions of those Opium dollars morphed (morphined?) into Bolshevik Revolution dollars in Russia and National Socialist (Nazi) dollars in Germany. All of this is one of the main reasons for Chinese hatred of the West, pre- and post-communism, this Opium trade. Again, the silence of the supposedly caring and compassionate fake media empires on this sinister activity screams volumes and can only mean that they fully understood, fully supported, and fully profiteered from it all. Sons have never been named after family losers, or family failures, or family misfits, or family lunatics. And when an exact name is passed down, it is the functional equivalent of God's writing Commandments onto stone tablets to be protected in an Ark for the remainder of Earth's history. In bagging four of the twenty blackbirds needed for the pie (family, legacy, diversity, and New World Order lunacy), all with one stone, Poppy's granddaughter Jenna Bush Hager, fake news woman for fake media empire NBC-Comcast-Universal, in 2015, formally birth certificated her second daughter: Poppy Louise. Yes, poppies to keep Middle Class Americans … losing … with ease. Sonny Bono wrote it right. The beat goes on. Addictions for American minds go on and on and on.

Old Bush, even by today's ever left leaning definitions, was never much of a Republican. Moreover, he was very definitely never a conservative. By now, even losers, failures, misfits, and lunatics have come to understand that any conservative mannerism had been a well-orchestrated act. That is a well-documented fact. Long before that, however, all the kinder, gentler, chuckling, pork rind crunching crud was also a well-orchestrated act. Back in the day, if anyone except for family members and bottomless pitted indebted insiders called him "Poppy," there would be a high price to pay. After said buffoon had his big foot removed from his big mouth, both the foot and the tongue would have been unceremoniously sliced off. But time and events and semi-free internet forced revisions to kinder gentler Bush tribe behavior. After WWII and his Yale Skull and Bones glory days, he moved his family to Texas, to try his luck in the oil business, which was not all that hard since it was in the oil division of his father's Harriman Brown Brothers international banking empire. Oh, sure, he could throw around some bull manure both literally and figuratively; however, like his father, old Bush was always basically a bought and paid for liberal Rockefeller Republican from the liberal Northeast wing of the party, just like Spikeless Ike, Bergen Belson Nelson, Junkyard George, Fool's Gold Goldwater, Tricky Dick, Boring Ford, T-Rex Ron, Floppy Sloppy Poppy, Doling Dole, Forging George Bush, Crash Cup McCain, Pit Stop Belly Flop Romney, and all the Republican clowns in Party's 2016 clown car. And, no, Cruz and Rand were not exceptions. Old Poppy had no time for Taft's balanced budgets, no time for McCarthy's unbalanced communists, and no time for Goldwater's hot water Cold War. The reason was secret just as the reason for his nickname Poppy was secret. The reason was that the prior 100 years, thanks to the Far East Opium

Trade, had morphed his father's and maternal grandfather's Main Street local mom and pop banking into a Wall Street international New World Order financial empire. Fake media empires glorified his extremely idiotic liberal social and economic policies, such as debt, taxes, deficits, inflation, wage and price controls, free rice to China, free wheat to Russia, more welfare for all. Poppy and his sons, including Jebberwacky, smiled and applauded JFK and LBJ. Later, Nixon, for all his law and order and free enterprise exhortations, never made a dent in crime or debt or inflation, nor did he make the trains run on time, unlike Mussolini. In his defense, no American President ever could, because every two years America has sometimes real sometimes fake elections somewhere of some kind for something, if not for President and Commander-in-Chief, then for Dissident and Bomb Thrower and Thief. Comedians cracked jokes about each new phase in Nixon's economic recovery plan, where folks stopped counting at Phase 50. Sickest joke ever: Nixon Supreme Court appointee Harry Blackmun wrote Roe v. Wade decision that legalized abortion in 1973. Poppy and his sons, including Jebberwacky, smiled and applauded. Both long before and long after Tricky Dick, all the SOP RINOs were just as tricky. In 2016 the American people were sick and tired of them all. And so was Donald Trump. Republicans had always kissed the backsides of socialists and liberals since WWII. Their reward was irreconcilable hate. They were all stupidly and terribly and traitorously tricky. Whenever they entered public office, at any level, and especially the Presidency, they kept moving, not to the right, but to the left. After all, the third most hated President in American history, RINO Richard Nixon, imposed on the Nation wage and price controls and treated Chinese and Russian Communist dictators as if they were old army comrades. The second hated President in American history, RINO Ronald Reagan, initiated the policies that started this illegal alien border lunacy and this immoral NAFTA trade and off shore and outsourcing lunacy. This lunacy was instrumental in the endlessly relentless and relentlessly endless deportation and exportation of American jobs, profits, pensions, and entire industries, once owed to, and once enjoyed by, the once Great American Middle Class, whose members died in wars. His speeches reeked of slippery promises that shed their skins when needed.

Pious Poppy and his sons, including Jebberwacky, supported Nixon in 1968, again in 1972, and Ford in 1976. When former Western film star Ronald Reagan started seriously running and preaching "conservatism," old Bush concluded the old cowboy had been thrown from horses one too many times, and cracked his Hollywood skull one too many times. As an aside, notoriously traitorous Supreme Court Justices appointed by Republican Presidents had been a miserably monumental monopoly since 1953. Spikeless Ike, after long and distinguished military and political careers, unlike any others in American history, was asked, at the end of his life, if he had any regrets. He finally admitted the appointment Californication Governor Earl Warren to Chief Justice of the U.S. Supreme Court was the biggest damn fool mistake he had ever made. When Old Bush lost his Texas Senate race both Nixon and Ford thanked him with various high level positions. Middle East dictators should have taken notes when Ford appointed him CIA Chief Spook. As many CIA Directors have stated the agency was never populated by choir boys and altar boys. It was never meant to be. Reagan had been kind of sort of gunning for the Oval Office since 1964, when after giving a speech supporting Republican candidate Barry Goldwater he gained nationwide acclaim. "Conservative" Goldwater repaid him by supporting Nixon in 1968 and 1972 and Ford in 1976 and 1980. Roped and wrangled and branded by reality, Reagan's conservatism was hanged high from a swinging rope before it ever had a chance. New World Order globalists forced Paul Laxalt off the ticket and Old Bush onto to it. After his serving as loyal VP and persuading Americans to read his lips long enough, Bush played CIA Chief Spook hard ball his entire Presidency to ensure Middle East oil, and all the Muslim terrorist homicidal fury that went with it, would explode inside the circle of the New World Order permanently. These new wars would never end. The phony slogan "New World Order" i.e., of liberty and democracy, became as normal as a new order of double cheese burgers and fries.

Old Poppy Bush's most Oscar- and Golden Globalist-worthy artistry was not acting like a conservative from the mid-70s to the mid-90s. It was since his days at prestigious Andover's Phillips Academy performing like a child-like, mild-Ike, Gomer Pyle-like, goofy, good guy, gallantly gliding through life without gall, grit, greed, or gumption. Born a couple months after cinematic craft-master Marlon Brando, old Bush perfected Brando's streetcars, waterfronts, godfathers, and last tangoes. Monty Clift, George C. Scott, Gene Hackman, and Jack Nicholson had nothing over Old Bush. He understood modern media as well as, if not better than, FDR, JFK, and maybe even Reagan. But not President Trump. Definitely not President Trump. Old Bush's grasp of the monstrosity of fake media empires came as no surprise. At Phillips he wrote and edited school newspapers and as class president political speeches. The millions that his paternal grandfather, maternal grandfather, and father made from Opium, The Fed, Bolsheviks, and Nazis taught him what to say, and what not to say, where, when, how, and why. His father had been on the governing body of Yale University and on the board of directors of CBS, the first, most leftwing, and most powerful fake news empire. His father, Shell game Sheldon, had known CBS founder William Paley since 1932. Ever since they shared holes in one and drinks at noon and schemes at night, away from prying eyes who would expose their hypocritical ones for all the world to see, and throw darts at. Old Bush while in the Navy spent more time killing time with Admirals and Marine Corps Generals than he did killing beers with fellow seamen. He married Barbara Pierce. She could trace her roots through distant cousins back to Henry Wadsworth Longfellow. Her father was president and publisher of Redbook and McCall's magazines. To call this Bush legacy an aw-shucks coincidence where Gomer Pyle moans "ggggaaaaaaaawwwwwllllllyyyy" was to call all the riots and protests and murderous rages after President Trump's election an aw-shucks coincidence

After war, college, and marriage, the first thing Old Floppy Sloppy Poppy Bush did was load up the family and haul them off to Texas and get into the oil business, with the blessing of everyone. In every interview then there was always the classic line about another young man going west to make his fortune. It took almost as long for folks to figure out who Bush actually was, and where he actually came from, as it did for folks to figure out FDR spent his Presidency crippled and sitting in a wheel chair, and JFK spent his Presidency crumpled after screwing Marilyn Monroe in her bedroom. Out of the world of crude oil and into the world of even cruder Texas politics, Bush kept rising through the ranks. While aching through Sidney Pollack's 1973 soap opera *The Way We Were*, with WASPy perpetual party boy Robert "Hubbell" Redford gliding grandly and gleefully through life and even into the screwy sack of Jewish communist rag writer Barbara "Katie" Streisand, it was difficult not to conclude the main character displayed various political roles of one George Herbert Walker "Poppy" Bush. Whenever asked he basically stated he wanted to occupy the most powerful office on the planet simply because it would be fun and new and neat. But Nixon, who had a hard earned reputation for political hard ball, appointed him America's UN Rep. Nixon hated the UN and demanded a definitively nasty SOB there. That long shelved character trait in Bush was the main reason Ford later appointed Bush to CIA Chief Spook. Please recall that many CIA men over the years have declared that the agency was not supposed to be populated by choir boys and altar boys. Such types fulfilled neither the mission nor the purpose. Old Bush, once President, would dump the mountainous manure pile of Gomer Pyle far into the past. Though Kuwaiti oil was less than a drop of water in an ocean, the remedy was war and New World Order. That term gushered off his lips more than all wildcat Texas oil strikes. Although the term implied liberty, democracy, and prosperity, our muslim "allies" were allowed to deny, destroy, and desecrate Bibles brought by our military men and women --- with swine piss and swine dung.

Yes, swine piss. And, yes, swine dung. The New World Order globalists lusted and muscled and hustled and rustled Old Cowboy Reagan's herds of cattle of the new conservatism right out from under his nose before he even hit the rawhide trail in 1980, when globalist rustlers hauled Paul Laxalt off the VP saddle and pushed Old Bush onto to it. Reagan spent his boyhood in a small Midwestern town in Illinois named Dixon, which this historian has visited many times. Extremely ice creamery Norman Rockwellian. Reagan saddled bagged that quaint main street culture with the Old West romanticized, ride and drink alone, white hat heroes in his fourth-rate movies. In another instance of life reflecting art, the fact is that his new conservatism was always more snake oil than motor oil. The New World Order globalists guessed he would not put up much of a fight, nothing like the streets of Dodge City or Tombstone. And they were right. After all, as Governor of the state of fruit cakes and nut cases (what else but Calipornia) in the late 60s and early 70s, the very first thing that Mr. Government-is-the-Problem did was … wait for it … raise taxes, growing the government, and screwing the Middle Class, and "trendsetting" for the other 49 states. In 1976 running for the White House, Reagan announced if nominated he would take as VP Richard Schweiker of Pennsylvania, one of the most liberal boneheads ever to sit in the U.S. Senate. Poor Reagan. He never rotgut whisky gripped the fact that his Rockwellian tangerine ice cream dreams would serve to churn Orwellian Big Brother schemes. For Old Bush and the New World Order globalists, the slogans were dignity, prosperity, liberty, and democracy. Yet President Opium Poppy Bush fully and unconditionally authorized America's united nations and muslim "allies" not only to keep pricing oil at "orderly" profiteering and middle class devastating rates, but also, and more importantly, to keep sliming The Holy Bible with swine piss and swine dung. One of the first questions this historian will ask when he meets His Maker is what He was thinking when the leader of the Nation, that was founded on His Word, His Law, His Truth, and His Wisdom, completely turned his back on All of Them.

Jebberwacky was the brother of George W. Bush (Forging George) (President Jan 2001 - Jan 2009). Both Forging George and Jebberwacky were the sons of Old Poppy Bush. It was telling that Forging George, the first born of Old Poppy Bush, for a middle name was given the last name of his grandfather's father-in-law, Walker, point man for Harriman's private international banking empire, and the millions of unseen unheard unknown of Opium dollars they poured into the American economy. Fake news empires always predicted young Kid Bush would be the perfectly punky party animal, the right wing's Bill Bonehead, but who could never run for anything, let alone win, not even West Texas tumbleweed sweeper. It is safe to say the list of terminally stupid and terminally snake oiled, led by the fake media empires, now includes but is not limited to druids, psychics, witch doctors, and astrologers, along with fortune tellers, tea leaves readers, tarot cards spreaders, and chicken bones throwers. Born in New Haven, CT, in 1946, one of the original baby boomers, Kid Bush came into the world a stone's throw from Yale's Skull and Bones Society building, in which both his father and his paternal grandfather became members. His moving, at the age of two to West Texas with his mother and father, so that his father could enter the oil business, was climbing on board a caravan to another country, but in his case legally. We are not so sure about his brother Jeb's wife's friends and relatives and Latino countrymen. For decades, the fake media empires had done such a Pulitzer Prize job sheltering Jeb's wife from the limelight that the only remaining question related to lime was how many millions of slices Old Bush and Kid Bush and Jeb Bush and the others in the tribe have shoved into their bottles of beer. And, of course, the brand was Mexican Corona. Mexico received money and publicity. The Bush tribalists privacy and loyalty. Hmmm. That patented formula emitted a familiar telltale odor. Bush became the fully-twanged, cowboy-booted, steak-chomping, beer-guzzling Texan. Rawhides and cattle drives and cattle rustlings, especially political cattle rustlings, exploded inside of and outside of young Forging George Bush.

By his own admission he tested his father's patience often. By admission of others he tested whatever was on tap to swill by the saloonkeepers, often, and whatever was on tap to swell in the saloonkeepers' daughters, more often. Too much corned beef, cabbage, and beer did not preclude Boston saloonkeeper Kennedy's grandson JFK from attending Harvard. In the same vein, thanks to grandfather Prescott and father George H.W. who had gone to Poison Ivy Yale, too much Texas WASP conservative Republican BBQ beef and corn on the cob, and similarly massive amounts of beer, did not preclude Dubya from attending Yale. Below average students through above average parents always up end it and end it up. Higher education in America stretched towards the Heavens in a two-headed goat or seven-headed beast from the sea sort of way. Approximately 20 years, 200 jokes, 2000 dates, and 20,000 beers later, by basic standard 1960s party animal calculations, after pre-Presidential and non-Presidential party animal battle with Bill Bonehead, Kid Bush made it the 3rd Bush Tribe generation in a row which would earn membership in Skull and Bones Society. Neither Society nor building is part of Yale. The structure reeks of medieval witchcraft, double reeks as Nazi Auschwitz extension, and triple reeks as

Stalin Gulag Grim Reaper monstrosity. Auditoriums had become crematoriums. Neither Society nor structure is subject to legal obligation to open door policies, or financial disclosures, or Federal Freedom of Information Act mandates, or any state, regional, county, or city mandates. There are also no legal obligations to be cozy with nosey fake news reporters or true news reporters or any kind of in between reporters. The ones that aren't in bed with skulls or bones or bonesmen are in dread of them. The Yale and Society relationship has always been mutually beneficial. Yale has received money and publicity. Society in turn has received privacy and loyalty. The privacy seemed easy, since the structure radiated (radiation?) all the grace and dignity of a medieval dungeon, or Game of Thrones torture chamber. Dragons flamed loudmouthed flesh into charred marshmallows.

Whereas Georgetown's baby booming Bill Bonehead was already plotting his drunken slut-humping road to the Oval Office, Yale's baby booming Forging George was simply plodding along. He signed up for the Texas Air National Guard so that he could switch back and forth rapidly and effortlessly between flying high in planes and flying high on booze. He bounced turbulently about from one thing to the next, a bit of this and a bit of that, a shot of this and a shot of that, spent time in the oil business, and went to Harvard and earned not one but two MBAs, one in Business Administration and the other in Beer Appropriation. Perhaps at the time DUI actually stood for Dubya Unhinged Inebriation. He was lucky to meet classic, elegant, delightfully lovely, and genuinely intelligent Laura Welch, also of Midland. Bill Bonehead would not be so lucky. He would meet and marry Hillary Rodham, known both then and now as Queen Hillary Artillery, who was exactly and exhaustingly and excruciatingly the opposite of Laura. Kid Bush was very lucky to marry Laura. She more than anyone for all things mature and for all things meaningful helped him cry up, dry up, flow up, and grow up. The birth of their fraternal twin girls a few years later guaranteed it. In this all-enveloping all-consuming media age, certain songs and certain Presidents go together, like eggs and bacon, or kale and tofu, whether desired or not, whether required or not. A few included Eisenhower and "Mame"; Bill Bonehead and "Don't Stop"; and President Trump and "You Can't Always Get What You Want." For

Oh Bonehead? "Unforgettable"? Forgettable. "Soulsville"? Splitsville. "Superfly"? Pooper scoop. "Billie Jean"? Peanut butter filled. Moonwalk was not mandatory because Oh Bonehead had 2 left feet, 57 states, and 5,000 teleprompters, which told him when to pick a knife, pour a beer, kiss his wife, and stare into headlights, like a deer. Oh, yes, and when to speak a "Michael" (!)(?) for his wife's Michelle's nickname real nice and clear. All applications in and all interpretations of logic, from Ancient Greek logic to Cosmic Vulcan logic, indicated Oh Bonehead's song was ... "Jive Talkin." What else for the original political Jive Turkey?

For Kid Bush, it had to be Country and Western star Marty Robbin's 1959 classic "El Paso" ... "out in the West Texas town of El Paso, I fell in love with a Mexican girl." Of course the year was 1977, the town was Midland, and the girl was British and French; however, the song was wet-eyed, the mood was starry-eyed, and the theme was rib eye steak and apple-pie. Like the girl's in the song, Laura's love was transformational, her loyalty multi-dimensional, and her and Forging George Bush's bond became indestructible and insurmountable. All men should be so lucky. Bill Bonehead certainly wasn't lucky. Not even Alpha Centauri star system close to lucky. That was 4 ½ light years away, at 186,000 miles per second. Readers are respectfully requested to do the math. There is no need to show the work. With her nagging and his whoremongering and their grubby-mitted grandstanding and smutty-ugly holier-than-thou reprimandings, the hang man's noose bond entangling the Queen and the Bonehead would always make them bobble and wobble at the edge of the abyss of suicidal and homicidal.

Kid Bush, both revitalized and solidified, marched forward as family man, business man, and political man, and, more often than not, political animal. Behind the scenes and inside the crowds he learned to soak up voter sentiments and presented them back to his father and Reagan to help them win in a landslide over Carter in 1980. After Carter's catastrophic cardigan sweater stunt, where he blamed middle class Americans for the misery of 12% interest rates and 12% inflation rates, Kid Bush absorbed his first big and lasting lesson in media nuance, when Reagan banned wearing sweaters and even sweatshirts by anyone connected to the campaign. He spent some time in the oil business. He almost did time in the jail business, not as a reformer, but as an inmate, for possible SEC insider trading violations. In some ways he proved as resiliently snake oil slick as Bill "Slick Willie" Bonehead. Besides, his father's father shell game Sheldon's banking activities funneling millions to dictators during WWII forced FDR to freeze some of his assets and to toast almost all of his ass. Kid Bush became investor, controlling partner, and general manager of the MLB Texas Rangers for almost five years. He and his family had a grand slam of a good time, watching a lot of home runs knocked out of the park, taking home a ton of money socked out of the game. He campaigned very little for Reagan's and his father's second term mostly because they really did not need it. He served as advisor for his father's first and only term as President in 1988. This would be the last time in a national campaign Republican Old Floppy Sloppy Poppy Bush would sell himself as conservative Republican. Forging George Bush, except for Texas-bred and Texas-twanged, was his father's son and his grandfather's grandson. His leaving his father's Episcopalian religion and liking his wife's Methodist religion persuaded him to talk more openly about fewer abortions and more prayers in public schools. But presidents and governors have little control in these areas. But the cheap publicity is priceless. Kid Bush learned to never take a stand unless you mean it. By now, even creatures on Alpha Centauri have heard about Old Bush's "Read my lips" line, which tolled the bell, and dug his grave. Reagan closed loopholes downwards and inched Social Security taxes upwards, and always as last resort. Old Bush raised middle class taxes almost automatically immediately. He thought he would be patted on the back for his compromises. Instead he was kicked in the can for his hypocrisies. Possibly he did not know. Probably he did not care. The second was to never let political clowns conduct a war. Leave it to real generals and real admirals. In the hell on earth Arab war with Saddam Hussein, Old Poppy Bush let him live at the advice of General Colin "RINO Clown" Powell. Globalist general consensus has concluded Powell, if he ever were to run, is one of the most, if not the most, qualified men to be Oval Officer in 2020. A fact never mentioned is that, a quarter century, 10 trillion dollars, and an ocean of American Blood later, that Middle East hell on earth is now more hellish than ever.

As soon as Old Bush stopped running, at the end of 1992, Kid Bush started running, to election day in 2000. He had started planning running long before that. The notion that frat boy party boy would never run for anything was more smoke and mirrors. The reason he ran was rudimentary: Revenge. Oh, sure, since Laura's love for him, he turned over a new leaf and burned down his old self. He guzzled less beer and dazzled more Lord. He boldly and soberly quoted from Leviticus and Proverbs to Romans and Thessalonians and the dawn of time and Garden of Eden virtues to leave revenge to God. But at 1988 Democrat Convention in Hot Lanta, blistering key note speaker Ann Richards, Texas State Treasurer, a whisky wacked out witch, a witch from hell and hate, vented with vulgar guttural gallows humor that Old Bush was not a true Texan, because he did not speak with a true Texas accent. And he did not speak with a true Texas accent, because he was born with a silver foot in his mouth. If the read my lips line was the most terminally stupid one that ever left Old Bush's lips, then Richards' silver foot in mouth line was the most eternally brutal one that ever left an enemy's lips. To declare Kid Bush life-or-death admired Old Bush was to declare largemouth bass life-or-death admired large lily padded and heavily weeded lakes and ponds. Kid Bush's boozed up outbursts in Midland could be heard from Maine to Yosemite. His mother almost slapped him silly and his wife almost smacked him bloody. To that point in his life, it could be argued that Forging George would never run for anything, including tumbleweed sweeper; after it, he would never stop running, including nuclear warheads code keeper. In the 90s while Queen Hillary and Bill Bonehead were winning two Presidential terms, where he was breaking cherries and campaign promises, and she was breaking rubies and health care systems; Kid Bush was winning two Texas Governorships, melting Ann Richards the wicked witch of the West (Texas), and belting would be Republican flying monkeys out of the skies and into their graves. He rebuilt both the Bush Tribe and the Bush Brand and indirectly the newfangled "conservatism" that had been built by Reagan. He had also served notice to VP Al Gore, to win the White House in 2000, it would take much more than dancing with druids, praying to pine trees, fumbling on rappers "F" bombs, sucking up to suburban soccer moms, and, most importantly, taking credit for the

Reagan-Old Bush economic recovery and prosperity. It wasn't that Bush was great; it was that Gore was bad. Both gruesomely and glaringly bad. Bill Bonehead was a natural. Few men south of the old Mason-Dixon Line in any profession ever did a better job of shoveling the political manure. He could lie out of both sides of his mouth, and sometimes his ass, all at the same time, both creatively and convincingly. After 8 years as VP, Gore still could not. Gore and his Democrats could never comprehend why more voters did not love him; Bill Bonehead knew easily and never campaigned for him. Predicted landslide victory turned into unexpected saloon defeat. Bush's Texas twang guaranteed him his home state plus the states south of that line.

Kid Bush never asked voters to read his lips. In fact he never asked his voters and supporters to read anything at all. They were just supposed to gulp down all his and VP Cheney's Halliburton and their New World Order steer manure on faith. His "compassionate conservatism" meant tax rebates of a few pennies per family and Federal deficits of tens of thousands of dollars per family. If his supporters had done some more reading, they would have learned Forging George's policies and intentions meant a mountainous pile of steer manure. Old Bush proved all too well that loose ones do indeed sink ships, and submarines, and aircraft carriers, and rowboats, and rafts. On the other hand, although Kid Bush was never willing to say "read my lips" in domestic affairs, he was more than willing to say "weapons of mass destruction" in foreign affairs, and once again in the Middle East, and once again about Saddam Hussein. And once again with the same predictable results. Centered and mentored by his VP New World Orderly Cheney, that devious POC and SOB from the Old Bush Administration who had assured America the "Peace Dividend" would balance the Federal Budget, save the whales, and cure the common cold, Kid Bush gave the Great American Middle Class a few pennies back in rebates and tax cuts. Those few pennies were horrifically offset by the Great Recession which began in late 2007. Kid Bush must have really "admired" his father Old Bush. Just like his father, he turned a 1982 Reagan – 1994 Gingrich solid economy into a bungled lobotomy. Just like his father, he sank America into a needless and winless and endless war in the Middle East. Just like his father, he made hell on earth would be more hellish than ever. Just like his father, he deemed both agreeable and irrelevant the final cost and the final solution: the ocean of American blood of soldiers and sailors and airmen; and the mountain of American gold and silver and precious stones. Liberals paid students and street bums to march with signs saying "No Blood For Oil." America never received any free oil, or cheap oil, or miraculously discounted oil. Not then. Not now. Both then and now Americans have always paid New World Order top dollar, globalist socialist Arab oil Cartel prices. Or perhaps the only thing more indefensible was the 2004 Presidential race where hard core Yale Numbskulls and Bonehead Society brothers Republican Kid Bush ran against Democrat John Kerry. If prior White House races had not proved America's two party system was a three ring circus clown act, then this one did. Boneheads put each other above all else, with blood oaths. Very few things were more disastrous than boneheaded wars for Arab democracy. Exceptions were boneheaded wars on African and Latino poverty. Huxley knew what Orwell and others did not. It never occurred to Orwell or others that perpetual wars were not merely conducted as military ones; they could more easily and more profitably and more justifiably be conducted for reasons of poverty, and snobbery, and dying trees, and health care fees, and illiteracy, and exclusivity, and mediocrity, and the Eater bunny, and the tooth fairy. Forging George Walker Bush, bottom line, provided forgeries on everything, except genuflection at, and supplication to, the altar of the New World Order.

Part IV – The Jebberwacky's Jumbo Joke

Jebberwacky, therefore, was destined to be moneyed, moderate, marvelous, powerful, influential, and Presidential. But his trip to The White House ended at The Out House. Thanks to Donald J. Trump. Those same fake media empires, that same smart money, those same beautiful people, and those same members of that vast, limitless, mad maximus, intellectual wasteland, that self-decreed and self-crowned artistic-political left, had declared new world orderly, that, well, okay, maybe Trump could somehow walk and talk and beat bums like Gilmore, jerks like Jindal, and punks like Pataki; and maybe, just maybe, he could out point Carson, Walker, Kasich, Rubio, and Cruz. However, there was no way Trump could beat the jabbing and stabbing and abracadabra-ing John Ellis "Jeb" Bush. Rock Hudson handsome, Norman Rockwell wholesome, and Kennedy-Rockefeller intellectually awesome, the Republican nomination was his to lose. Like his older brother Forging George, Jebberwacky spent his boyhood in Midland and went to school at Andover Academy. Unlike his older brother, he never roared at rodeos, and he never rode the rawhide. In fact he rolled a barn load of reefer, and he ranked a wagon train of low grades. Afterwards, in 1970, he and other Andover students climbed into vans and caravanned down to Mexico, to build a school, where he himself taught English. As Americans had been doing for over two centuries, Jebberwacky and buddies went to help those who seem to be the eternally hopelessly chupacabra-out-of-luck poor. Over 200 years of American driven, proven, ventured and uncensored liberty, democracy, industry, technology, and Protestant Christianity had done little to alleviate global lunacy, poverty, stupidity, and illiteracy. Slowed by Catholic molesters, Communist dictators, New World Order International banksters, on most continents things stank JFK sleazier, LBJ uglier, and Jimmy Carter nuttier than ever.

They had to. Somewhere along the line the word "Work" had been meticulously deleted from the principle of "Protestant Work Ethic." Fake media empires had transformed it into enslavement to the slothful. To suggest otherwise would be to ignore God's recorded Word and fundamental Truth. Thousands of years ago, in the 15th Chapter of Deuteronomy, God declared: "For the poor shall never cease out of the land." Two thousand years ago, in the 12th Chapter in Gospel of the Apostle John, to Judas Iscariot the Betrayer, Jesus Christ The Master and The Redeemer declared: "Let her alone: against the day of my burying hath she kept this. For the poor always ye have with you; but me ye have not always." Modern Christians by the millions around the globe had become convinced that Jesus had descended to Earth, not to reveal He Himself was the only Way, Truth, and Life to His Father, which Jesus stated clearly and forcefully in that same Gospel 4 Chapters later, but to preach the practice of lunacy, stupidity, perversity, vulgarity, and rampant blasphemy, in all their forms, and to roll a perpetual printing press, to dole out an eternal supply of global welfare checks. All this was due to 150 years of potent ongoing brainwashing by fake news and fake entertainment empires. They have all been owned and controlled, with strangleholds, through fake people: atheists, agnostics, communists, socialists, or, in other words, leeches, loafers, parasites, bloodsuckers, kooks, crackpots, maniacs, and murderers. od made it even more obvious than ever that those who should be helped, and only those who should be helped, were widows who were truly widows, and orphans who were truly orphans. Women were created to bear children. Men were created to bear burdens of their wives and children and bear weapons of war and protection against those who dared destroy city walls. Paul made these points in the 5th Chapter of his First Letter to Timothy. Paul wrote it a few years prior to the Roman Empire's destruction of Jerusalem and Second Temple in A.D. 70.

Paul knew both tragedies would occur sooner rather than later. Nationally he was born a Roman citizen in Tarsus, Turkey. But religiously he was also born a Jew and raised as a Jew in Jerusalem. He also was educated on and familiar with Greek, Persian, and Egyptian cultures. When he travelled on the road to Damascus, God chose him then and there because few men or women knew these groups, especially Jews and Romans, inside and out, more shrewdly and more intuitively. Paul concluded if the Roman Empire or Jewish Nation did not destroy or at least dismantle to an irrelevant degree the tenuously toddling new religion called Christianity, well, then, the new free loaves and fishes forever mentality of the new Christian assemblies definitely would. Reports reached Paul and other leaders, from Rome and Corinth to Galatia and Jerusalem, indicating a rapidly expanding majority, where one and all were simply sitting around all day long, staring at the sun, studying the acts and works of the Apostles, and waiting for manna to fall from Heaven and for mead, wine, "other strong drink," and juice from "forbidden fruit" to pour out of rocks, if not flood out of mountains. Paul was nearing the end, of a saintly post-conversion life where he had been thrown to sharks and thrown into prisons and fought the good fight and finished the race --- all for Christ.

Timothy, in charge of the church at Ephesus in Turkey, sought Paul's leadership. Paul responded with the first letter. In it, especially at the end, Paul's pre-conversion Pharisee traits asserted themselves:

> But she that liveth in pleasure is dead while she liveth. And these things give in charge, that they may be blameless. **But if any provide not for his own, and specially for those of his own house, he hath denied the faith, and is worse than an infidel"** (emphasis added). "Let not a widow be taken into the number under threescore years old, having been the wife of one man, Well reported of for good works; if she have brought up children, if she have lodged strangers, if she have washed the saints' feet, if she have relieved the afflicted, if she have diligently followed every good work.

Paul's use of "he" and "his" and "house" and "infidel"; and their context; and their impact; must be measured and resurrected culturally and spiritually. If 969-year-old Methuselah or 29-year-old Timothy, from first page to last page of the Holy Bible, "infidel" was the worst possible damnation and denunciation. At the time of Christ, "infidel" contained the same weight and intent as it does now for Radical Arabian-muslim Terrorists (RATs). As for "house," HBO's *Game of Thrones* series still provides the best current working definition. "House" was not a small one or two parent, one or two offspring family. "House" meant spouse, in laws, children, grandchildren, menservants, maidservants, farmers, tailors, hunters, and soldiers. Earlier than Paul, 4,000 years earlier, Moses shows Abraham's battle to save Lot. New King James Version (NKJV) of the 14th Chapter of Genesis is provided for the benefit of younger generations and more fully defines "house"; "Now when Abram heard that his brother was taken captive, he armed his three hundred and eighteen trained servants who were born in his own house, and went in pursuit as far as Dan. He divided his forces against them by night, and he and his servants attacked them and pursued them as far as Hobah, which is north of Damascus. So he brought back all the goods, and also brought back his brother Lot and his goods, as well as the women and the people." Lot was of course Abraham's nephew but "brother" is used here by Moses to emphasize the proximity and intensity of this relationship. At the time of Christ, a husband and father had a legal, practical, financial, and religious duty to and responsibility for his immediate families, and extended ones. For leaders of the New World Order, the round the clock denunciation and obliteration of the Protestant Work Ethic would be followed by the new theology of Jesus extoling doling out free weed, free booze, free ribeye steaks, and free baked potatoes; or perhaps free kale, free tofu, and free avocadoes, from Mexican drug cartels, who use the cash to stash and dash more illegal murderers across the borders into America.

Jebberwacky proved no exception to modern propaganda that had transformed modern practical Christianity and global government bureaucracy into mutual admiration societies and mutually reinforcing monarchies. Fake media empires kept selling the idea that money grew on trees. Many modern Christians, like him, kept buying it. In a way it was easy, since he and many like him had never touched a hammer, or nail, or metal lunch pail. Even imams, rabbis, priests, pastors, ministers, and the Pope himself, bought it, hook, line, and sinker, or maybe crook, blind, and stinker, with end goal of all those opposed ending up blind and leading the other blind into pits of pity, stupidity, and mediocrity. All the members of the fake media empires did not care, since they always made damn sure almost all the tax loopholes were formulated for and beneficial to themselves, their cronies, flunkies, groupies, and floozies. All the while they made it sound as if the problem were big oil, big coal, big iron, and big defense. Their lives would always have plenty of private profiteering to red brigade, red carpet, black caviar, and pink champagne their lives of revelry, perversity, and vulgarity. For many, ignorance is bliss; for guys like him, it seemed almost imbued at birth. He went to Mexico, built schools and houses, laughed and lounged, sang and drank, and befriended men who behind his back thought him simply another American fool. He came back for more and to do more and met and later married Columba Garnica Gallo, who was 100% Mexican, and, more importantly, 1,000% for full unconditional amnesty for all illegal border crossers into America, at any border, north, south, east, and west. A woman's love does strange things to a man; sometimes an overripe rescue gene is unleashed; in his case, he became unglued and obsessed, to the point where he wanted to "save" not only all Mexicans but also all Latinos around the globe, with Middle Class American Tax Dollars.

Jebberwacky, overburdened and overshadowed by his father and his older brother, attempted to establish his own identity and personality. He passed on Yale, tennis, and baseball, and Numbskulls and Boneheads Society. He enrolled U of Texas and cheered at Longhorn football games, where the school had an outstanding program under Head Coach Darrell Royal, NCAA wizard of the wishbone offense. Jebberwacky and others in stands perfected the rah rah rah hook them horns symbol, with fore and pinky fingers protruding high and wide, and with middle and ring fingers curled and pulled in tight by the thumbs. Millions still do not know this was an ancient Babylonian devil worship symbol rebrewed by medieval warlocks and witches and more recently by rock stars, movie stars, and Satan worshipers like Aleister Crowley and Anton LaVey. All of a sudden, inexplicably overnight, college kids were using the horned devil symbol at Longhorn football games. Some readers may think that is just more steer manure. But few a years earlier, San Francisco acid rock band Jefferson Airplane members in album and publicity pics used the same horned devil symbol, which made perfect sense, since they spiked with and crashed near Church of Satan High Priest, the goateed Anton LaVey. Some readers may think that is just more Tim O' Leary Lucy Skies. But a few years earlier, across the country and the Atlantic Ocean, in the Muslim bought and paid for London-Dumb, a young rock studio guitarist crowned Crowley his king, raked licks for Donovan's tune *Season of the Witch*, and Jimmy Paged his way to fame and flames down Satan's stairs Inferno-ly. Jebberwacky may have been a better actor than his father and brother combined. He may not have taught others through a Numbskull and Boneheads secret society card, but similarly he sure taught the Great American Middle Class exactly where the cattle prod was poked. And, now, in 2018, when people watch the Oscars and Golden Globe Awards, celebrities protrude that damned horned devil sign more often than they high five, bump fists, and vomit F bombs on The President.

Jebberwacky, to maintain his faking of a kinder, gentler, more compassionate conservatism, whatever on God's green Earth those Bush bumper stickers meant, passed on marrying a Mayflower-rooted New York City Episcopalian as his father had, and he passed on marrying an English-French-rooted Texas Methodist as his older brother had. He married a Mexican Catholic woman and converted to her faith, both religiously, and, more importantly, as voters were to learn decades later, politically. He put both Connecticut and Texas in the rear view mirror and moved his family to Florida, not because of fatherly guidance, brotherly advice, or business career, but because his wife already had relatives in Florida. Like his father and older brother he tried some of this and some of that, not too high, not too low, not too fast, not too slow, biding his time, timing his strides. Like all New World Order Globalist Socialists left and right and in between, he was both dumb and dumber at the same time, but he was not stupid. He entered and departed oil, banking, real estate, and investment firms. He campaigned for his father both VP times and both Oval Office times. He did not have his brother's tempest in a teapot dome scandal temper. But he also did not have his brother's Mephisto-phallic-ly fake Texas twang. During the Ann Richards summer of 1992 drunken ramblings about Old Bush's silver footed, golden booted, iron toed, iron heeled heart, mind, and soul, Kid Bush went bonkers; whereas Jebberwacky went artistic. He barely lost the Florida Governorship 1994, won it by the same margin in 1998, and won it by a few more in 2002. He was winning most moderates, most conservatives, a little under half the Jewish vote, and a little over half the Latino vote. He cut taxes and regulations, and improved health care and education. Fake media empires and experts and followers declared confidently that the 2016 Republican Presidential nomination, through this new political coalition, was his to lose.

The polls said, by late 2014 and early 2015, Jebbberwacky would obtain his party's blessing almost universally unopposed. His believing them was his first monumental slab of trouble. Perhaps the only thing stranger than political bedfellows is fake media empire truth gallows. In late 1963 and early 1964, the polls said George "Junkyard Dog" Romney (yes, the father of Mitt "Pit Stop – Belly Flop" Romney, that "civil, somber" Mormon with the newly minted mouth of a New Testament legion of demons) and Junkyard Dog's new progressive Rockefeller Republican policies would: beat first LBJ then Goldwater; make his hokey, smoking, choking AMC Ramblers better than a Rolls Royce; and transform Detroit into the Garden of Eden. In 1972, the polls said Dummycrat George McGovern would beat Richard Nixon, just before Nixon won in a landslide, where to this day those reporters are still stunned since they and all friends had voted for McGoofy. In 1980, 1984, and 1988, the same fake media empire polls said the same fake things about Dummycrats Carter, Mondale, and Dukakis, against Reagan twice and Old Bush, with same results. In 2016, the same polls said Queen Hillary Artillery would beat crotchety crackpot communist Bernie Sanders by at least 33% in the state of Michigan and lock up the Dummycrat nomination, just before sanders won. The same fake polls, of the same fake media empires, owned and controlled by the same fake people, with the same fake hearts, and same fake minds, and same fake souls, said Queen Hillary Artillery (and her lap dog Bill Bonehead) would beat the bobbing, heaving, dancing, weaving, floating, stinging, counter-punching, bounty-hunting Donald J. Trump. But Jebberwacky was earning raises and praises and accolades and Gatorade and along with all the other Bushes was burning those who raised eyebrows about his burning bush policies and abilities. Jebberwacky was branded fast learner, good listener, smooth speaker, and strong campaigner. These were commendable qualities for any profession, be it professional politics, or professional ping pong.

However, for Jebberwacky, who announced his candidacy on June 15, 2015, none of this was remotely close to the truth, just like Forging George Bush's Texas twang before him, and just like the reasons for Old Poppy Bush's nickname before him. Fast learner? In the early '70s, he had no basic position on, let alone consistent policy applications to, the War in Vietnam, often talking out of both sides of his mouth, and sometimes his butt. Decades earlier former Dummycrat President Bill Bonehead proved to be a mesmerizing master at these two kinds of talking. But we are discussing the intellectual toddler, Jebberwacky. Around 20 years later, he had exactly the same position, doing exactly the same kind of talking, about his father's war in the Middle East. This war was for the free flow of oil. But there was never anything free about it. Not then. Not now. The higher the amount of American blood that was spilled, the higher the price of Arab oil that was drilled. The true purpose of the war was to make the phrase "New World Order" as normal as "ham and eggs." Around 20 years later, Jebberwacky had exactly the same position, doing exactly the same kind of talking, about his brother's war in the Middle East. Hearing Forging George ramble and stumble, most Americans have concluded that WMD really stood for Words from Mumbling Dimwit. It is hard to say if the reason was cultural, educational, or biological, but of course mostly a joke of a combination of all of them, with different parts of each to larger or smaller degree at different times. Jebberwacky needed weeks to try to explain himself. Like most baby boomers, he thought himself supernatural since he and his fellow buffoonish baby boomers somehow "survived" what has obviously been the greatest era of liberty and prosperity and opportunity in human history. That luck, family, and dynasty, and sophomoric sense of supernatural ability, explained how a professional man and a professional politician can go his entire life without learning to explain his positions on the, not one, not two, but three, horrific foreign wars that he had witnessed in his lifetime.

Good listener? Jebberwacky's father the former President and his brother the former President had told him since the 1960s, when they all supported George Romney, Nelson Rockefeller, Nixon, and Ford, neither Goldwater nor Reagan, that it was no longer possible for a Bush to fake being conservative. Old Poppy Bush had made the phrase "New World Order" as common as the "common cold." Forging George Bush had made the phrase "Skull and Bones" as common as the "common man." Jebberwacky's mother had told him to stay in Florida and wrestle with alligators, not Dummycrats. His wife and children had told him to stay in Florida and peel the rinds off oranges, not the skins off terrorists. His For the past half century, and especially the past quarter century, the Great American Middle Class had grown disgusted, both Black Plague sick and 600-year-old Noah tired, for having been slavishly forced, both by bayonets and by bazookas, to heal and feed and clothe and shelter every Arab or African or Latino or European or whoever else crossed the borders illegally, or remained in the country illegally, or had been forced fed illegally by the fake media empires the lunatic notion that all the ills on the planet were somehow the fault of the Great American Middle Class. Jebberwacky had no comprehensible clue. In fact in his standard speeches he stated all the illegal immigrants, ie., Muslim terrorists and Latino MS-13 gang members and African warlords, came as an act of love. Oh. Sure. That was like saying the Nazi Gestapo threw humble harmless Jews and Catholics and homosexuals in the death camps, as an act of love. His final solution was no border walls, with full amnesty, and full citizenship, for all of them. Then double all middle class taxes at all levels. Yes, a woman's love can do strange things to a man, to the point where his entire soul is robotically obliterated. His political action committees raised --- and Jebberwacky spent --- $140M. According to fake media empires like the Washington Post that earned him … listen … listen … listen … a détente-like 3 delegates.

Smooth speaker? When millions of Americans who considered supporting him heard of the amounts of money Jebberwacky was raising, they concluded of course that he had the debating skills of Homer the ancient Greek. It turned out he had the skills of Gomer the modern Pyle. When they concluded he had the speaking skills of Saint Paul in Rome, it turned out he had the skills of a Saint Bernard in Nome. When you turned on the television and tuned into the Republican Presidential debates, Jebberwacky's performances made a first timer at a high school debate look like Socrates. He was the great-grandson of Samuel, insider to oil empires; he was the grandson of Prescott, insider to bank empires; he was the son of George H.W., U.S. President and insider to Skull and Bones New World Order; and he was the brother of George W., U.S. President and insider to Skull and Bones New World Order. And all Jebberwacky produced and presented was jumbo jibberish. He was reduced to sparring with Rubio combo Grouch Chico Harpo, as if outpointing that empty-headed empty-suited dumbo slightly right of center would earn him the nomination. But just as Rubio had no clue he was in the same category, Jebberwacky had no clue that the fake media empires were helping him win. As soon as he did, and ran against Queen Hillary Artillery, they would destroy him and his "new coalition" as just another Darth Cheney evil empire Republican. There were so many running and debating, for the longest time there was a first team and a second team. The fact of the matter is that Jebberwacky should have been the very last brain-rattled, glass-jawed, cauliflower-eared, Styrofoam-spined chump allowed in the ring, if at all. Perhaps he thought actually going out on the campaign trail, actually talking to real Middle Class Taxpayers, with real Middle Class fears, from Albany to Albuquerque, from Chicago to San Francisco, was beneath him, as he passed judgement from his tower, on the peasants, whose privilege it was to have another offspring from the Numbskulls and Boneheads Society sit on the throne, be it gold, or silver, or ivory, or perhaps iron.

Finally, strong campaigner? Trump called him Low Energy Jeb for a reason. And that stayed in the minds of the American people for a reason. They knew, and believed, exactly what Trump meant: both low ability and low mentality. So let us take a deeper, more detailed, more deep state examination of the raw numbers and raw dollars. They say that numbers do not lie. But in politics they often do. But in Jebberwacky's case the numbers were not only terribly true but also abysmally brutal. After 7 months and 5 days, he suspended his campaign on February 20, 2016. More accurately the voters terminated once and for all the Bush Tribe from conservatism, from the Republican Party, and from the American political system. Or so they thought (see Robert "New World Order Mule" Mueller III and his deep dark state of Numbskulls and Boneheads). The numbers were painfully plain and catastrophically clear. Depending on the fake news empire of choice, Jebberwacky never spent less than $100 M and never won more than 4 delegates. New York Times in June 2016 said $162 M and 4; Center for Responsible Politics / Open Secret $155 M and 4; Time / Money in Feb 2016 said $150 M and 4; Washington Post in July 2016 $150 M and 3; The Hill in July 2016 $150 M and 3; Wikipedia $138 M and 3; MSNBC $130 M and 4; Washington Post in Feb 2016 $124 M and 3; Politico $103 M and 4; CNN $100 M and 1; and Reuters $100 M and 3. He must have lost 1 at the convention and Lord, er, make that Marx and Lenin only knew how and why CNN came up with 1 only. Again, regardless of fake news empire of choice, he never spent less than $100 M and he never won more than 4 delegates. He ended up spending no less than $25 M per delegate or as much as $54 M. In terms of Presidential politics, in fact in terms of all politics, that had to have been the worst return on investment (ROI) in human history. That made the Great Depression look like 1,000 shares of International Banksters stock (meaning the full faith and credit of the U.S. Government backed-Federal Reserve backed (meaning the full faith and credit of the debt-slaved Great American Middle Class backed)) stock bought in the early 1910s; or 1,000 of McDonald's and Coca-Cola in the early 50s; or 1,000 of Walmart and Gulf and Western in the early 60s; or 1,000 of Harley-Davidson and Berkshire-Hathaway in the early 70s; or 1,000 of Apple and Microsoft in the early 80s; or 1,000 of International Banksters in the early 2010s. Ah, yes, death and taxes and the New World Order --- those three definitively fake Lords --- were the three certainties in life. The noose around the neck and jive around the jugular problem was that Jebberwacky and his merry band of New World Order misanthropic marauders for the past 100 years had been enslaving the American people with the same return on investment when it came to the Nation's peace and prosperity, and especially the once great American Middle Class. Jebberwacky's Presidential campaign ROI made the mountain of trash from one million illegal immigrants in one year that jackass joked about seem like a mountain of gold. His race ran out of hope, out of time, out of money, and out of any connection to reality, past or present. His broad generalization came from too few samples; he concluded the America of 2016 was like the Florida of 1996, or his wife's Mexico of 1966. He really thought his new coalition of rice, beans, bagels, tofu, and oranges was going to replace the basic conservative menu of steak, mashed potatoes, and apple pie; and sometimes fried chicken, biscuits, and gravy; and sometimes cheeseburgers, hot dogs, and bratwurst. Jebberwacky was dumb but he was not and is not stupid. Neither are the other members of the Bush Tribe. Neither are the McCains and Romneys and Ryans, aka Crash Cups and Flatman-Splatmans and Boy Blunders. In 1917 after the communist revolution in Russia, devoted boneheads became commissars, and bootlicking clods and back stabbing slobs who could not read or write became KGB Colonels. In the brave new world, of the new world order, men and women were dumb, and dumber than dirt, but, they were in charge, and they had the hearts and souls of monsters and demons.

All his political consultants and all his high-priced handlers, fatally afflicted with political hoof and mouth and intellectual foot in mouth disease, merely move on, like his New World Order allies, without missing a note, without skipping a beat. Presidents and Oval Office Wannabes and their signature songs have been discussed. Jebberwacky never became President. He never became Commander-in-Chief. He never will. But he does have a song. Only God could have known that, when Richard Rodgers and Oscar Hammerstein II composed the classic musical *Oklahoma!* in 1942-1943, it would contain a song for a politician born 10 years later in 1953. Only God could have known it would summarize succinctly that politician's demise 53 years later. The musical remains unchanged. The song's music remains unchanged. However the title required updating to *Poor Jeb is Dead,* and the lyrics also required updating as follows:

Poor Jeb is dead
Poor Jeb Bush is dead
The Trumpster stole, right back, our ice cream cones
Jeb hungered iron grip
On wicked White House whips
Could not be gamed and throned by skulls and bones

Poor Jeb is dead
Poor Jeb Bush is dead
His views are more extinct than dodo birds
The people are afraid
Illegal crossings made
And so he seemed a dorky clueless nerd

Poor Jeb is dead
Poor Jeb Bush is dead
It's clear for years that he's been out to lunch
He deems us mangy mutts
Then slices up our guts
And now we know he always spiked our punch

Poor Jeb is dead
Poor Jeb Bush is dead
He could not sense the quicksand of his past
He thought his tune was sweet
Dried concrete his left feet
To Davy Jones he sank Titanic fast

Poor Jeb is dead
Poor Jeb Bush is dead
His globalists sent back to drawing boards
The Federal Reserves
Perhaps have lost their nerves
Comes Alpha and Omega Two-Edged Sword

Poor Jeb is dead
Poor Jeb Bush is dead
He must return to distant asteroids
He's cracked from head to toe
Like Larry, Curly, Moe
No opioids can cure his hemorrhoids

Jebberwacky ran a below average campaign for an average politician. He ran a mediocre one for a moderately successful former Governor of Florida. He ran a cataclysmically amateurish one for the establishment choice to battle the ruling Queen and brutal Commissar, Queen Hillary Artillery.

All Jebberwacky-style dynasties must rest in peace.

And in pieces.

Part V – Queen Hillary Artillery: The Brutal Ruling Commissar

The Ruling Queen and Brutal Commissar, one Hillary Artillery, would grab the gonads of one Donald J. Trump and flame him to ashes in her gulag. Her William Clinton Bonehead's floozies lay flat upon their backs, just itching to insert attacks. She would out think him, out talk him, and out point him. Yes, Trump had met his match. Once again, the fake media empires, the smart money, the beautiful people, and the members of that vast, mad maximus, intellectual wasteland, the self-decreed and self-crowned artistic-political left, all stated confidently and new world orderly that Trump was an overlord, an underdog, and, therefore, an afterthought. She would knock him around the four corners of the ring, and then knock him around the four corners of the globe. She would knock him up to the search lights, and then knock him down to the lowlights of the lightweights. She would cut him up like a kale and tofu and avocado salad, chew him up, spit him out, and, finally, toss the imprecise and impetuous Trumpster into the local city dumpster. Once again, the fake media empires declared confidently that Mr. Trump might have been able to enter the 2016 Presidential race, and he might have been able to remain in the race, and he might have been able to surpass all the braindead Republicans, and he might have been able to survive the onslaught of Jebberwacky and the Bush Tribe and the New World Order. However, there was no way on Darwin's Bolshevik's Earth that The Donald could ever overcome the Queen, and, yes, the New World Order. Remember, always remember, the New World Order owns both political parties. The hollering was a hoax; the campaigning a crock; the bickering all proverbial bunk. Except for Trump. The NYC Donald Trump of 2016 would NOT be the NYC Joe Namath of 1968. Arrogant guarantees are for the gridiron, not tire irons and iron horses. No Deep State Way. Queen Hillary Artillery, the Entitled Empress, the Ruling Queen, the Brutal Commissar, was the smartest woman on the planet, or maybe in the universe.

However, Master Planner, Master Builder, Reigning Champion, and our American President, our Donald J. Trump, knew, both shrewdly and intuitively, that Hillary, a baby boomer like himself, had spent the first third of her life as sort of a feminist version of Jeb Bush, the next third of her life as sort of a feminist version of Ted Kennedy, and the current third as sort of a feminist version of Manchurian ivory tower flower power. The prior two decades, and especially the last two years prior to the 2016 Presidential election, she seemed to change stances and positions on issues and policies more often than she had changed her hair styles. Aside from the fact that no basic standard left thinking feminist would be caught dead worrying about the shape or length or color of the strands of her hair, Hillary's hypocrisy portrayed a classic poster child of a miserable, unsatisfied wife, in a miserable, political marriage, to a miserable, boring, whoring, boneheaded bum, where the wife is perpetually pretending to be someone else, something else, and somewhere else. To the average 21st century American feminist, if the man in her life was concerned about the public beauty of the hair on her head, there was no way the idiot was ever going to be permitted to see enough to be concerned about the private beauty of the hair between her legs. When she wasn't laughing herself silly at the sight of his insect-sized dick, she would be laughing herself even sillier at the moves of his amoeba-sized mind. Yes, definitely pathetic. Not only was Trump the only Republican candidate smart enough to sense that all this Hillary smartest-woman-on-the-planet garbage was, well, garbage, he was also smart enough to keep this fact to himself. He would need these and other brass knuckles facts hidden in his gloves to counteract and counterpunch against all the extra brain-rattled bums that would be permitted in the ring to help her. Trump had always instinctively known what very few others on the planet knew, or if they knew what they were afraid to state: Queen Hillary Artillery, without 500 staffers and researchers and United difference between William Clinton, Clinton Eastwood, Woodrow Wilson, and Wilson Pickett, and maybe Picket Fences.

Walls? On Borders? Why would she and fake media empires be so totally opposed to border walls? Massive walls and gates and fences and barriers, both physical and philosophical, for unity and society and sovereignty, have existed since God expelled Adam and Eve from the Garden of Eden. Adam was obsessed with Eve's not always forbidden fruit flashing between her legs. Eve was obsessed with God's always forbidden fruit hanging on the tree. And, so, Adam and Eve were both expelled. And they were never permitted to return. In every picture since, God's iron gates close hard and fast and smack them both on their backsides on their way out into the real world. The ancient 12 Tribes of Israel, Aztecs, Chinese, Sumerians, Babylonians, Solomon's Temple, Christ's Jerusalem, the Vatican, and others all had or still have walls or barriers erected to protect them. Perhaps the only thing older than walls is the perfectly normal instinct of self-preservation of the people inside walls. Moreover, here in America over the past 100 years, the fake media empires have done a marvelous job building walls to keep their people in and well-protected and to keep all others out and unprotected. Put on your coolest rapper best, and try moonwalking into that hard left rag of newspaper New York Times, or that hard left snuff of a filmmaker ATT-WarnerMedia-HBO, and demand word-for-word reports and scripts and sexually subliminal picture-for-sexually subliminal picture, for intense scrutiny by all conservatives and nationalists of all shapes and sizes and colors, and see how far you get. Nowhere. Fast. If those in charge do not show you to the exits, you can be sure their trigger-ready guards will. Better yet, try striding boldly and patriotically into one of their MK-Ultra Secret New World Order Globalist conferences, at a Bohemian Grove, or Bilderberg Resort, or Rockefeller Estate, and you will be stopped, in the way a lake of fire stops a drop of water, by the biggest, meanest, ugliest, grubbiest, most gruesome gorillas on the globe. These thugs, these Philistine Goliaths, make HBO's GOT's Sir Gregor Clegane, aka The Mountain, in full battle armor, look like the munchkin children in MGM's 1939 classic *Wizard of Oz*. The Mountain could not make the cut.

Hillary Diane Rodham was never the smartest woman on the planet. She was, however, since her college days at Wellesley, possibly the most pampered, most protected, and most publicized. She was born after WWII in Chicago and brought up in its middle class suburbs. Just like Jebberwacky, she was bred as a liberal Ike-Nix-Ford-Reagan (until 1960, Reagan was a devout FDR Democrat)-Bush-Dole-Bush-McCain-Romney-Rockefeller Republican, soying and toying and enjoying all of America's post-WWII prosperity. Urban legend and her own boozy muddy memories maintained she somehow managed to escape a neo-fascist household and neo-Nazi neighborhoods. That was fanciful nonsense, needed decades later to win the votes not only of hardcore feminists, but also, and more importantly, of practical, suburban, culturally conservative leaning soccer moms. Both the era and the area reflected and reinforced her liberal wing Republican cultural and political views. Besides her own Illinois Percy-Dirksen civil rights influence, other major influences included, like a compass pointing straight north and then moving methodically clockwise like a classic mahogany grandfather clock: the Robert La Follette progressive movement in Wisconsin; Ford-Romney-Rockefeller coalition in Michigan; Beveridge scholarly tradition in Indiana; Kem corruption free movement in Missouri; Hickenlooper Marshall Plan and United Nations policies in Iowa; Kellogg-Thye drug and food health legacy in Minnesota; and Ike's war time General and Presidential accomplishments stemming from his boyhood days on the family farm in Kansas. Hillary's father was neither the boozer nor the wife and child beater both she and the fake media empires have implied for the past 50 years. Her two brothers were not older and bigger and nastier, but, in fact, younger and sillier and quieter. They became committed, if not formally registered, Dummycrats long before she ever did. One served in the Peace Corps and married a Cuban immigrant who taught total amnesty. The other worked for an unknown Bill Bonehead and later married California's U.S. Senator Barbara Boxer's daughter. This historian by accident witnessed Ms. Boxer in the early days up close and personal. For all those under 40 years of age, please note Boxer made crazed, occult-like, Santeria-smitten Alexandra Ocasio-Cortes, the notoriously bar-tending-bred AOC seem singing nun sweet and serene and sensible. Most of this Rodham family history had occurred before Hillary learned the difference between Mississippi River's muddy waters and Chicago blues king Muddy Waters. Her muddy memories made sense digging his music and smoking all that weed. All the Hillary the Nazi Hunter nonsense ranked right up there with the dashing, dancing FDR; sober, studious JFK; praying, spraying Peanut Butter Brain; and wonky, STD-free Bill Bonehead. As for Oh Bonehead, he was all sludge murky and jive turkey.

The middle third of her life, duplicating Ted Kennedy, the younger, louder, dumber, drunker brother of JFK and RFK, heir to the throne of Camelot, seemed to make a lot more cents, a lot more sense, and a lot less sitting on the fence. By the time she graduated from Wellesley in 1969, she had become a fully committed Feminist, registered Democrat, and devoted New World Order Globalist Socialist. She howled her way into Poison Ivy League Yale Law School, dopily hoping to dig up some inside dirt on Numbskulls and Boneheads Society, since she entered Yale Law School the year after Kid Bush had graduated from Yale University. Both stiff and stuffy, she clawed her way as a staff attorney onto the shyster assassination squad of the U.S. House Committee, originally intent on the personal destruction of President Nixon, through Watergate, or water cups, or water drains, or whatever water was available, where, in the end, the fake media empires pissed all over him, as well as all over the American people who had re-elected him in a historic landslide. There was a Constitutional crisis, for "democracy." The 68 million dollar question for the 68 year old Hillary Rodham after all the decades was not how the fake media empires destroyed President Nixon, after he in the prior five years gave them and their socialists everything they had demanded. President Trump, it should be noted, was not the first one to have a bull's eye painted on his back for New World Order bazookas. Rather, the question had always been how she bawled and clawed and carved open a spot for herself onto that Watergate committee, since there were millions of young women who were immeasurably smarter, braver, tougher, livelier, prettier, sturdier, more learned, more endearing, and more deserving. She and Bill had not yet become the new darling duo of the Rothschilds, Rockefellers, Bilderbergers, and Bohemian Grovers. In her youth, the "smartest" woman in the world had already proven that she never had been and never would be. Had her tissue paper thin skin, ego, and virginity, been unceremoniously poked by some sick hypocritical joke of a man, just like the no good bum she had married? Some sick hypocritical Hollywood Clown? Fascist? Communist? Professor? Numbskull? Bonehead? Bilderberger? Bohemian Grover? How, where, and on whom did she obtain the appropriately obligatory deep state dirt to steal an insider's ringside seat? Back then, as now, a gal like her, both uptight and uptowning, both boring and overbearing, didn't simply strut panty less in faded blue jeans, braless in rainbow tie-dyed T-shirts, drive a flower power-stickered VW Bug to DC, park it in a lot, and park her butt next to Watergate Scandal Special Prosecutors Archibald Cox and Leon Jaworski. It did not work that way then, and it did not work that way now. Both then and now, millions of young women would have sold their souls for that desk. Millions did, along with other body parts, and they still failed. Something had happened to Ms. Hillary Diane Rodham. Some scumbag. Or scumbags. Who was or were wealthy, powerful, and influential enough to keep her big mouth shut for almost four decades, with payoffs here and there, starting with the position of staff shyster on that Nixon Impeachment Committee, and potentially ending in and with the Oval Office. But since her wet-behind-the-ears-and-wet-between-the-legs Watergate days, she has always come up short. After decades of mocking men, spitting hate, freeing their inner b****, she and millions of women just like her have finally "found" themselves, forced to kneel before, and depend on, men like her boneheaded scum bucket of a husband, to win the White House.

Hillary Rodham then inched her way oh so dangerously, oh so defeatedly, and oh so deplorably, up to the altar to marry her Bill Bonehead, would be Commander-in-Chief, Commander-in-Leaf, and Commander-in-Thief. During her marriage to him, he would achieve all three, not necessarily in that order, but always by and in and for the New World Order and their Orderlies and their Hordes and their Whores. Conversely, she would achieve none of the three, although she would try more foolishly and frequently. They exchanged vows. She gave him white lace, garter, sunshine, and promises. He gave her night waste, Sartre, moonshine, and syphilis. Blind men, and even never say die feminist sisters who ate up all the smartest woman on the planet garbage, could see that as soon as she had clutched his loins and coattails she regretted it, called a shrink, and fixed a drink. And another.

And another. So, sadly, as things supposedly seemed at least in the public eye to get "better and better" both personally and professionally, like Ted Kennedy things seemed to get worse and worse, and she began to drink more and more, both personally and professionally. Things went from worse to worst after loving and lusting in and leaving Chicago's Metro area, Boston's Metro area (Wellesley), New York City's Greater Metro area (Yale Law). Balled and chained to Bill Bonehead, who was not remotely related to her emotionally, she had to move for all practical purposes south of the old Mason-Dixon Line to Arkansas. Arkansas is a lovely state with whitewater rapids, white cedar trees, and deep dark caves. It has never been easy, especially for women, despite all the media empires propaganda, to move from big city America to small town America. To move, from cosmopolitan Chicago, Boston, and New York, to small town Arkansas, is almost impossible. Depressingly for Hillary, the move must have been from Queen's Royal Court to deepest and darkest primitive cave. And now she shared a bed with a man who had the balls and the blood of a primitive cave dweller. And this man's only gift was the ability to talk, at the same time, out of both sides of his mouth, and sometimes his ass. Years decades later she would feebly offer that she followed her head and not her heart. To which all Americans muttered "What heart?" It was something out of standard definitive Hollywood bull manure. At least the Tim Man openly admitted he had no heart, but she would not. At least the Tin Man openly admitted that he wanted a heart, but she would not. School marm handy at Rose Law firm, drool charm brandy on the campaign trail, and cool arm candy for her Arkansas Governor husband, Bill Bonehead, she felt the best years of her life melt away, like the wicked witch of the west, or, perhaps, like ice cubes in her highball glass on a hot, sticky, Arkansas August night, where mosquitoes bigger than crows sucked your blood, where her glass burst to overflowing, with one-quarter orange juice, and three quarters vodka.

In January 1993, Hillary Diane Rodham's current third of her life kicked into high gear. But her and Bill Bonehead's Globalist Rolls Royce choked and smoked and stank and cranked more like one of Junkyard George's and Pit Stop – Belly Flop's old AMC clunker Ramblers. Please recall that, in the late 50s and early 60s, Junkyard

George, every bit as left as Queen Hillary and Bill Bonehead, drove the State of Michigan and City of Detroit straight into the ground and down to the 9th circle of economic hell. Please recall also before that he drove American Motors Corp (AMC), which was gearing up to be the next Tesla, down to exactly the same place. Please recall also that the fake news empires were crowning Junkyard George as the next wunderkind, who would save all Americans from the likes of Nixon, Reagan, McCarthy, and Goldwater. Please recall, finally, that monumentally moronic Mitt, in the past 50 years, has not uttered one damn word of apology for his old man's monumental failures. Not one damn word. Both Bill and Hillary ramblered due to their gasoline diluted with water due to their and their Globalists' obsession with elimination of cars and trucks. Gender generational finger pointing has already appeared at its worst on the left. Both Ms. Ocasio-Cortez, barely out of her toddler pampers, and Ms. Rodham, barely into her old witch's hag pampers, in the greatest nation the world has ever seen, are consumed with mean, bitter, entitlement lunacy. In 1993 Hillary stormed into the White House as entitled First Lady, brutal Commissar, and ruling Global Queen. Her bonehead husband, Bill, with rocks in his head and boulders in his toes, reeking of booze and floozies, entered the White House as U.S. President, New World Order's Rolls Royce Dent, and Horny Swine for Rent. For two decades in Arkansas, which for her had been the other side of the universe, she had doubled Bill admittedly superbly as eggs to his ham, brain brandy to his arm candy, and sounding board to his diving board. He spent his married life screwing almost anything in skirts, except Hillary. She spent hers stewing in a universe of hurt, without exceptions.

Hillary Diane Rodham: First Woman President. Queen Hillary and Bill Bonehead. Those words have a nice ring to them. Bonnie Elizabeth Parker: First Woman Bank Robber and Machine Gunner. Bonnie Elizabeth Parker and Clyde Chestnut Barrow. Bonnie and Clyde. Those words also have a nice ring to them, in fake media empires kind of way, since they had made two gay freaks, Cary Grant and Rock Hudson, sex symbols, for women, along with a ton of money. For all practical purposes, Queen Hillary was already the first woman President as Co-President with Bill. They say behind every powerful man is a powerful woman. The Queen had the Bonehead in her cross hairs, by his short hairs, and, as First Lady, she would have the most famous, amorous, and glamorous styles of hair, each week, at $500 a pop, all at Taxpayer expense of course. On the one hand, Bonnie grew up Texas cactus poor, both rejected and neglected, yet turned out Snow White dainty and pretty. She attended schools from hell for free that that failed, that left her dreadful and frail. She loved Clyde Barrow and praised the Earth on which he walked. She gave him loyalty and treated him like royalty. Due to her poor education, she did not know thing about politics, economics, New Deal, or Federal Reserve. But she did know and she made it point to Clyde that they would only rob banks that had made money during the Great Depression charging grave-digging usury to the almost poor and plainly poor. In the end, after a lifetime of crime, law men riddled Bonnie and Clyde with enough bullets to supply American soldiers in WWI, because the law men did not have the balls or brains to riddle the real criminals with bullets. On the other hand, Hillary grew up Chicago suburb upper middle class, both pampered and protected, yet turned out Wicked Witch scary and surly. She attended schools like Wellesley and Yale, that left her resentful and stale. She hated Bill Bonehead and cursed and pissed the rooms in which he whored. She gave him vulgarity and treated him with hilarity. Due to her Poison Ivy Leagues education, she knew next to nothing about politics, economics, New Deal, or Federal Reserve, just like "uneducated" Bonnie. But she did know and she made it a point to Bonehead that they would only rob the Taxpayers that were being robbed by International Banksters. It did not matter if International Banksters doing the robbing were Jews, Hindus, Shintos, Sunni Moslems, Shiite Moslems, Catholics, Protestants, Atheists, Agnostics, Fascists, or Communists, as long as they were robbing Great American Middle Class Taxpayers. New World Order bank men and law men showered Hillary and Bonehead with enough billions to pay off the National debt. Real law men did not have the real balls or real brains to riddle the real criminals with real bullets. History has already proven Artillery Hillary's weaponry to be bloodier, costlier, and deadlier, and more profitable. Bonnie and Clyde. Rodham and Bill. America has reached the point where queens and boneheads are serving, not law, not order, but New World Order.

For Queen Hillary and her Bill Bonehead, Dramatically Undynamic Duo (DUD), into the White House, the past 25 years have been marked by one horrifically humiliating failure after another. For former Co-President Hillary Diane Rodham, and her on again off again drunk again whore again husband, former Co-President Bill Bonehead, their time has been spent in henhouses, cathouses, doghouses, outhouses, brewhouses, and, 5% of the time, in penthouses. That 5% is what the fake media empires have devoted their entire empires to over the past 25 years, at 365 days, 24 hours, and 60 minutes, just ask the fake news fake folks at 60 Minutes, at CBS (Cyclops Bread-robbing Secrets). There were times here and there when Big Brother wasn't watching, but there were never times when CBS (the CNN of the 50s, 60s, and 70s) and their false gods brothers and sisters were not. It had less to do with consumer habits on shampoo and toothpaste and mouthwash; it had more to do with wham bam who and trash waste and brainwash. The first, the most boneheaded, and still the most notorious failure was Co-President Hillary's --- Her Majesty Queen Hillary's --- health care program. It contained all of Oh Bonehead's health care program's failures, plus a few more. Hillarycare was sired in political cloaked and daggered back rooms and born in political emergency room and died almost immediately due to genetic and biological defects. She ran around the country hollering women's rights are human rights, but not in the medieval Moslem countries where Old Bush had fought his war. In those countries, whose cousins here always voted for Dummycrats like Bill and Hillary, women's only right of any kind was the right to have their femininity sliced off with sabers or flamed off with torches by "deeply religious" Moslem men. Nor did she run around hollering here at home in places where the women her husband raped or abused cried and died. Those women had the right to stay in their poor white trash trailer parks and set themselves on fire in trash dumpsters.

The easily predictable negative effects of Old Poppy Bush's 1990 tax increases on the Middle Class, which Dummycrats like Queen Hillary and Bill Bonehead front and center had demanded, and the Federal spending and deficits of Oh Bonehead's 16 years later, which made her and him worse than Ebenezer Scrooge, rapidly sank the economy to the worst in 50 years, like the kind they had blamed on Old

Poppy Bush. The economy sank so brutally so rapidly, that Republicans in 1994 under Newt Gingrich captured the majority in the House, for the first time in … wait for it … 50 years. It is hilarious (Hillarious?) how peachy how politics can present the same number with such poetic justice. To clunker in their rambler into the White House parking lot for a second term, she and Bill accepted welfare reform and welfare-to-workfare programs from Mister Newt and his conservative Republicans. To the hard left, hard core, hard ass, hard head socialists that she and Bill needed, these programs were worse than volunteering for Nazi "work" camps. At least the Nazis gave those volunteers bar soap, whereas welfare-to-work folks were required to buy their own. Oh, wait. As VP Al Gore and his wife had done to stoke Bible Belt supporters, Queen and Bonehead bragged her Protestant Methodist girlhood and adopted a more religious tone and stance, until Monica Lewinsky genuinely genuflected to their version of Babylonian god in the flesh, staining and maintaining all sorts of tones, stances, gyrations, and adorations. Fake media empires wrote around the clock begging Americans to believe that being whoring horse's ass had nothing to do with being a lordly President. That saved her skin, and what was left of her Bonehead's venereal disease-ridden "tricky dick." Again it is hilarious (Hilarious) how politics can provide poetic justice. She wrote a book about how it takes an entire village to raise a child. Common Sense Middle Class Americans pointed out that, if America is her village, well, then, she lucked out and ended up in the White House due to millions of village idiots having the right to vote.

Co-President Queen Hillary exited Chicago's Muddy Waters – Saul Alinsky culture, Wellesley, Yale Law, and, now, the White House, in exactly the same she had entered them, as nowhere near the smartest woman on the planet, but definitely the most pampered, most protected, and most publicized. She was not finished. She would always have the New World Order Emperors and their Orderlies padding her streets and credentials and patting her butt and potential. She carpetbagged her way to the U.S. Senate through New York State. In that lunatic logic that Dummycrats utilize in so many areas, she implied her days at Wellesley and Yale were close enough, especially, as they say, for Federal Government work. Readers are invited to think back to their worst experiences at their local U.S. Post Office. As Senator she failed because she never even tried. She gave the basic thumbs up to all things left, theft, wacky, and welfare; thumbs down to all things right; and thumbs in her mouth alone at night to hide her insurmountable insecurities. The fake media empires, the smart money, the beautiful people, and the members of that vast, limitless, mad maximus, intellectual wasteland, known euphemistically as the self-decreed and self-crowned artistic-political left, all stated confidently and new world orderly that soon, very soon, she would first official woman President in 2008, the coolest and hippest and smartest woman. Ever. But she had not planned on Oh Bonehead. He was not supposed to run until 2016. It became more important to vote a Black Man over a White Woman into the White House, even though he turned out to be even dumber, more pampered, more protected, and more publicized. But, he might have had a better memory. He was sworn in as President Oh Bonehead on (His Koran? Colin Kaepernick's Koran? Iran's Official State Koran? Mecca's Museum's Koran? His Bible? Martin Luther King, Junior's Bible? Abraham Lincoln's Bible? Martin Luther's Bible? Who knows? Who cares?). Oh Bonehead immediately remembered the lesson, for party unity, from his political uncle, Boston's U.S. Senator Edward Kennedy, about his brother JFK, yes that JFK, in 1960.

Oh Drunkard told Oh Bonehead how his brother JFK brought on as VP the hated LBJ of Texas. Oh Bonehead made Queen Hillary (and her Bill Bonehead as background) Secretary of State. She became his Sanctuary of Slate, his be all, end all, cure all, in foreign affairs. Oh Bonehead also remembered from the 1990s Bill Bonehead's lesson on cabinet secretaries. They are never page turners nor rage burners, but they are always fame makers and blame takers. The boneheaded debacle at the U.S. Embassy in Benghazi, Libya, where Ambassador J. Christopher Stevens and three other Americans died was, well, nothing less than a boneheaded debacle. Oh Bonehead, Queen Michelle, Bonehead Biden, his wife, insiders, nearsiders, even administration farsiders, even her husband Bill Bonehead, scurried into the rotten eggs rotten in Denmark reeking darkness, like gutter rats at the witching hour in a slummy alley in a Chicago ghetto. Oh Bonehead left himself angling with a win and left Queen Hillary dangling in the wind. Queen

Hillary had always hungered to run and hunt and piss with the big dogs, and, now, after all the decades of loyalty, after all the decades of slavery, after all the decades of humiliating humility, she saw they all were sprinting, from her, after they all had been pissing, on her. To rescue her, fake news empires buried and carried and hurried and scurried. They tried to say this was nothing like Nixon's Watergate scandal. They tried to say that was a Constitutional crisis. In the real world of love and hate and tears and pain and life and death, the difference was that in Watergate a few opposition research files were found and shredded. Whereas, during the Benghazi tragedy, real living, breathing, drinking, eating American Citizens were found and shredded. With their own karma completing the circle, the Presidential victories themselves were failures. Queen Hillary and Bill Bonehead had the lowest percentage of the popular vote for the winner since Woodrow Wilson in 1912. So, for her 2016 race, her past 25 years, both personally and professionally, could be succinctly summarized in one word: DEPLORABLE!

Hillary Rodham Clinton: First Woman President. Not only of the Tax America To Death Party, but also, and more importantly, of the Blame America For Life Party. To the Obamas, Clintons, Carters, Johnsons, Kennedys, Trumans, FDRs, Wilsons, up-and-comers, down-and-outers, and in betweeners, and all the others, this seemed exceptional logic: blame the Great American Middle Class, forever, and tax It to death, forever. Yes, officially, in 2008, and again in 2016, she angered and hungered to become America's first official woman President. However, unofficially, she would not, since she already had been. Effectively President when Bill sat in meetings and signed documents and shoveled the horse manure (Jan 1993-Jan 2001), behind closed doors she exercised the brains of the operation and executed the power of the institution. Each time he predictably pulled out his prick she systematically stacked more tons of mortared bricks of blank check blackmail to her castle walls. The only health care he had ever wanted centered six inches below his waist, ensuring at proper time and place the flesh protruding six inches hard and straight for the next Presidential porking of any woman not named Hillary. But she wanted her political love child born wild to be "affordable health care" for all citizens, but especially for all women for free birth control, free morning after pills, and free abortions, at any time, at any place, on demand. So he obeyed. But they failed. The health care program called Hillarycare would be born in a hospital emergency room and after much suffering died almost immediately due to severe genetic defects, especially brain defects. Oh Bonehead's version would survive but only at the expense of an arm and leg of the members of the Great American Middle Class who were forced to pay for it. As for President Bill Bonehead, that famously phony, swinishly horny Whoremonger-in-Chief, who could go from southern small town drawl to northern big city hip like a light switch, well, the only glass ceilings he ever cared about existed as P.T. Barnum-manufactured mirrors in the Presidential Suites of the swankiest 5-star hotels, for reflecting his drunken cocained perversions with women and the deliberate ruination of their lives. But she demanded the immediate shattering of the remaining few corporate glass ceilings preventing promotions for and opportunities to deserving women. So he again obeyed. But they again failed. The only clean water he ever cared about needed to be perfectly pure mineral waters, supposedly preferably French Perrier's, that went into his ciders, lagers, bourbons, moonshines, and whatever else he had downed over the past quarter century that produced his present state of "dead-head-stalking-dead-Prez-walking." But along with her Hollywood hypocrite communists and Ivy League stinkweed socialists she demanded laws requiring toilets to be flushed only once a day, teeth brushed only once a week, and showers taken only once a month. Farm animals watered only once a week. Any resultant laws would have required all citizens to be equal, but she and her cronies and comrades, in that observation about communist dictatorships by George Orwell, knew they would always be more equal than others. So Bill again obeyed. But he and she again failed. Bonehead's success, ability, and 65% approval rating, both then and now, were all phonier than his in faith in the 50 pound Bible he carried around during his Monica Lewinsky Impeachment days. The Queen and the Bonehead, after 25 years of new world order failures on the world stage, succeeded at standing up and taking credit for the successes of others, almost always Republicans, such as the elimination of Federal deficits in the 1990s and the elimination of Arab terrorists in the 2000s.

During her heavyweight championship bout with our President, in the summer of 2016, with the fake media empires in the ring, defending her to the death, doing almost all of the punching for her, Commissar Clinton stated recently that, if elected in November, she would tap into husband Commissar Billmonica's prior economic expertise, so that the economy during her Presidency 2017-2025 would produce the same solid economic success 1993-2001, when he reigned as King, and she reigned as Queen. Of course, she reigned as Queen inside the royal court. Everywhere outside of it, as everyone knew, which meant outside of the Washington D.C. beltway and outside of Democrat Party inner circles, she "reigned" as Court Jester-ette. She knew this herself, patiently playing compliant wife and underling to Boneheaded Bill's horse's behind husband and overbearing overlord. She tolerated nearly matter-of-factly short term gender deprivation and marital humiliation in a profitable exchange for long term political coronation and historical glorification. Potheads, potholes, and all sorts of pot shots had impeded her progress to immortality, first with Bill, then Obama, then Sanders, and, finally, Mr. Trump. However, now, thanks mostly to a super screwy Democrat delegate allocation system, and an equally super screwy Media information dissemination system, Mrs. Clinton saw it all, within her acrimonious grasp. Her use of "tap" went completely unnoticed, even among the wackiest rightwingers. Thus "tap" entered the Nation's lexicon as one of the most, if not the most, monumental Freudian slips ever to escape a political woman's lips. In their marital lifetime Bill had already flamboyantly bamboozled more floozies than a galaxy's worth of bed bugs in a Thailand drug cartel's house of prostitution. She herself had been in charge of locking down the lid and hiding bimbo eruptions during the 1990s. With $126M-plus in Wall Street Profiteering speeches excluded, for poor little Hillary's Hegelian indestructible yet spontaneously combustible psyche, "tap into" meant: With a cattle prod ... Into his venereal-disease-ridden prick ... And she would keep tapping into them ... Tapping into them ... Tapping into them ... Until he produced verifiable and quantifiable results. With any other woman and in any other circumstances, "tap into" would have been taken at face value, as another way of reclaiming the blue collar – coal miner trust she had heartlessly discarded into city dumps, or saying "relate to"; "connect with"; or "feed a pipeline within." But not with her. And not in these.

Queen Hillary Artillery failed to practice, let alone perfect, Bill Bonehead's impressive assortment of acquired and inherited personal and political skills. The most important one might have been his affable ability to glad hand and withstand and be all things to all people and to support simultaneously policies mutually exclusive, depending on audience. He always talked, and still talks, out of both sides of his mouth, and sometimes out of ass, and all at the same time. One week he talked criminal justice reform to Harlem Blacks, the next week he talked crime control to NYC's finest men in blue, and both groups walked away convinced he had their backs. To this day, when he travelled south of the Mason-Dixon Line and east of the Rio Grande River, his smooth drawl mesmerized, moving like warm honey over corn bread in the heat of the summer in the Southern Appalachians. LBJ started it, Carter maintained it, and Bill Bonehead perfected it. Almost as good were two lads who came into the world as WWII babies from Liverpool, formed a musical foursome in the late 1950s, and used the most modern scientific subliminal techniques to sell, literally, lonely white kids on their artistic and musical originality and superiority. One died from gun shots at the hands of an MK Ultra nut case, and the other one's average concert ticket price could pay off the UK national debt, for songs written yesterday with help from friends back in the old U.S.S.R. on long winding roads, where jojo mojo salted, peppered, and buried minds. True revolution meant no solutions. True Christianity meant mind-altering, drug-defining idolatry. Bill Bonehead had witnessed them take that mind game, come-together, imagine-no-possessions, give-peace-a-chance stance. All the way to the bank. Eight days a week. He found them royally hip and triumphantly rich. Bill Bonehead had a natural and nurtured sense of humor. Queen Hillary Artillery had natural and nurtured senses of anger and resentment and entitlement. Sometimes it seemed she was the only person on the planet who did not know those traits would not a local election for dog catcher.

Perhaps the second most important one at which she failed might have been Bill Bonehead's ability to accept pats on the back and strokes of the ego, and of course on and of other body parts, for successes that resulted from policies he had initially resolutely opposed. He boasted like carnival barker and strutted like a professional wrestler. After he and Hillary had obtained the required stamp of approval from Trilateral, Bilderberg, and International Banking groups, he started running for the Presidency in late 1991, and never stopped. No Powercrat ever stopped running for office, even after he or she had left office, or even after he or she stopped running for office, i.e., Al Gore for clean air and private jets; Jimmy Carter for homes for peanuts; John Kasich for erroneous polls and Ohio mailmen; and Jeb Bush for right wing versions of Tweedledum-dum Ted Kennedys. Commissar Hillary, appearing at a CNN town hall in Columbus, Ohio, Queen Hillary Artillery promised that in her administration: "I'm the only candidate which has a policy about how to bring economic opportunity using clean renewable energy as the key into coal country — because we're going to put a lot of coal miners and coal companies out of business, right, Tim?" She then smiled the biggest, dumbest, dorkiest smile in the history of American Presidential politics at the town hall audience. She added: "And we're going to make it clear that we don't want to forget those people. Those people labored in those mines for generations, losing their health, often losing their lives, to turn on our lights and power our factories. Now, we've got to move away from coal and all the other fossil fuels, but I don't want to move away from the people who did the best they could to produce the energy ...." Since she had never lifted a shovel in her life, except maybe to bash Bill Bonehead in the head after one of his notorious and well documented escapades with a slut, she had no idea how unbelievably dumb her statements were. After that, despite fake media polls, she could never really dig her way out of the bottom, unlike the coal miners she had addressed, who had spent their lives doing just that to advance the industrial revolution and the strengthen the industrial base of America. In early November she announced a $30 Billion plan to ensure that coal miners and their families get the benefits they've earned and respect they deserve, to invest in economic diversification and job creation, and to make coal communities an engine of US economic growth in the 21st century as they have been for generations. But such empty promises were too little too late. As then-Candidate Trump, other conservatives, and even many Democrats pointed out, the idea that coal miners in southern Ohio and West Virginia were going to make solar panels for minimum wages was sillier than circus clowns. Solyndra jobs lasted a few months, but they cost taxpayers about half a billion dollars, due to wasteful boneheaded subsidies by President Oh Bonehead, that she had extolled as the future of energy.

In West Virginia, coal miners traded their shovels and pick axes and lighted safety helmets, and rugged mountaineers their boots and bloodhounds and Remington hunting rifles, long enough for booths and ballots to vote for Trump. While halfway across the country in Nebraska, hog and beef butchers traded their knives and meat cleavers and storage freezers, and corn and wheat farmers their silos and diesel fuels and John Deere tractors, for the same to do the same. Then men went back to work. Then women went back to work. Then those without some work went back to seeking work. They had no choice. They felt pain about the recent past, fear for the future, and frustration regarding the Nation's direction. However, according to all the exit polls, these men and women, young and old, left and right, black and white, the heart and soul of the American Middle Class, felt as if they had been knocked on the head, kicked in the gut, and stabbed in the back, by establishment politicians, on both sides of the aisle, in both parties, who had spent years and sometimes decades, and always their hard-earned tax dollars, promising peace, harmony, stability, and prosperity. They took those hard-earned tax dollars, and, after stabbing Middle Class Americans in the back, went behind their backs, scheming to kill the meat industries and coal industries. When Commissar Hillary's hundreds of handlers staged a town hall meeting in West Virginia to pump up her eerily slipping poll numbers, a young coal miner family man showed up, gave a picture of his family to her, and asked with admirable respect why she wanted to make millions like him jobless, and their families hungry and homeless. Back in early March she screamed she going to put a lot of coal miners and coal companies out of business. Very few politicians in American history have so matter-of-factly told millions of Americans that she was going to literally terminate their entire industries, and their children, and their grandchildren. Clearly the red leaning Commissar Hillary Artillery ended up caught, red handed.

The smartest woman on the planet seemed to have the mind of a lobotomized amoeba. Hilarious Hillary inadvertently provided whole new dictionary definitions to terms like "shovel" ready projects. In the end, she dug her own grave, and Trump knocked her and all the fake media empires right into it.

Autumn, 2018

The Front Door Whores and Back Door Wars

Part I

President Trump serves America not only as President but also as Commander-in-Chief. On the other hand, both handily and back-handedly, Obama was Propogander-Money-Launderer-in-Chief; Kid Bush was Skull-Bones-Blander-in-Chief; Clinton was Whoremonger-Tail-End-Pork-Hers-in-Chief; Old Bush was NWA-CIA-Expander-in-Chief; Reagan was Not-So-Innocent-Bystander-in-Chief; Carter was Nutty-Cardigander-In Chief; Ford was Putty-Rocker-Flander-in-Chief; Nixon was Red-Russia-China-Rubber-Bander-in-Chief; LBJ was Steer-Manure-Candor-in-Chief; JFK was Slit-Spreader-Slammer-Slander-in-Chief; Ike was Good-for-Goose-Gander-in-Chief; Truman was Jerry-Merry-Pander-in-Chief; and FDR was Pearls-Swine-Middle-Class-in-Meat-Grinders-in-Chief. The Heaven-fearing and freedom-revering sagas and spirits of our Original Founding Fathers of our Original 13 Colonies have nearly been terminated by those 13 pretending Presidencies --- aka Putridencies. Both the hearts and the souls of the members of our Great American Middle Class have nearly been terminated by those 13 bartending, goaltending, globe-tending, needle-and-spoon-tending, and New World Order-spending Commanders-in-Chief --- aka Commanders-in-Grief and aka Commanders-in-Thief. Those plodding and imploding Putridencies, explain primarily, if not exclusively, why things have gone from bad to worse, if it were possible, since their international bankers' Federal Reserve's Great Depression. Yes, there are now two fruit smoothies in every kitchen; two organic chickens in every pot; two free range beef roasts in every oven; two kale-avocado salads in every fridge; two tofu barbecues on every grill; two cell phones in every bathroom, two computers in every bedroom, two widescreens in every living room; and two electric cars in every garage. However, this "progress," no matter how broadly and benevolently and beneficially defined, has come at an astronomical cost. The ancient Biblical eye for an eye at Leviticus 24:20 (KJV)? This 20th and now 21st century "good life" demands both eyes, both hands, both arms, and both legs, of both parents, at three jobs, each --- at slave wages. Worse, most of the slaving away was, and still is, done for city, county, state, national, and global freaks, leeches, loafers, lunatics, and freeloaders. The members of our Great American Middle Class are the ones President Trump is determined to make great once again. Nearly forever they have been buried in graves after lifetimes of being enslaved by invasion, starvation, condemnation, humiliation, debt, taxes, deficits, inflation, and immigration, both legal and illegal. The members of that Great American Middle Class are the ones who have paid for trillions of dollars of bread and butter; beer and weed; welfare and warfare; and rockets' red glare and cupboards bare and Obamacare and Bill Bonehead's affairs.

For all that "progress," those 13 Presidents themselves did not pay those astronomical costs, out of their own personal funds, facts both legally certified and Federal Reserve verified. No. It was not FDR and his fireside chatting chips; it was not Truman and his whistle stopping popcorn; it was not Ike and his golfing pal cocktails; it was not JFK and his revolving front door whores; it was not LBJ and his longhorn cow pies; it was not Nixon and his law and order soap operas; it was not Ford and his global banksters and his whip-inflation-now buttons; it was not Carter and his peanuts and cardigan sweaters; it was not Reagan and his jelly beans and cowboy hats; it was not old Bush and his New World Order Orderlies; it was not STD Clinton and his begging single moms' kindergarteners to pay off the national debt; it was not young Bush and his fake Texas twang and cattle rustling border wall promises; it was not Obama and his bankrolling his Radical Arabian-islamic Terrorists (RATs) brothers in Iran, with $1.5 Billion in Great American Middle Class Taxpayers Cash, without the approval of the Senate, Supreme Court, or House of Representatives, or, most importantly, without the approval of Great American Middle Class Taxpayers. Even most liberals agreed that kind of money doled out to that kind of enemy required the review and approval of American taxpayers themselves. Oh sure. Like Robin Hood pinching sixpence from ribald members of royal courts in the British Empire's Sherwood Forest at the time of the Crusades, here and there those 13 Presidents pinched some pennies from the empires of men like Bell, Edison, Morgan, Stanford, Carnegie, Rockefeller, Gates, Buffett, and Zuckerberg. Unlike Robin Hood, those 13 and their IRS Commissars, both Sheriff of Nottingham indoctrinated and KGB inebriated, spent most of their time stealing from the Great American Middle Class. Nonsense about "wretched huddled masses yearning to breathe free" on the Statue of Liberty was primarily designed to start driving down wages, keep driving them down until reaching pre-Civil War slave levels, load The Nation's cemeteries with plenty of dead, debt-slaved Taxpayers, and bloat The Nation's treasury with plenty of dead, debt-slaved Taxpayers' tax dollars. Again, even most liberals agreed that, if anyone should be consulted by an American President to dole out global welfare and global warfare to global bankers and local scumbags, it is those same Great American Middle Class Taxpayers. It was a damned and depressing fact of life in America that President Trump seemed the very first President to feel so, to think so, and to say so. Benjamin Franklin is more famous for stating the only two sure things in life are death and taxes. He never thought a person would die directly from taxes due to working around the clock to pay for those who did not work or did not pay taxes. Oh, well. John, Paul, George, Ringo, Dingo, Gringo, go home, but Jude can't make it bad, since Lucy had kaleidoscopic eyes, but please let it be yesterday's pepper spray.

The KGB and Gestapo bred and guttered and bread and buttered owners and controllers of the artistic-political left and their world-wide media monopolies needed to replace Stormy Daniels. A new show was needed, new slogan, new savory flavor of the month. The stormy, the slutty, the wormy Ms. Daniels, the new poster child for all things Democratically moral and morally Democrat, needed to be trash canned through a new script to disrupt President Trump's Presidency and popularity. Tossing lies and fakes and clumps and chunks of weed and meth, like P.T. Barnum's clowns tossing taffies at his sucker-born-every-minute circuses, modern media clowns, for the 2nd time in a little over year, had propped and photo-shopped the front door whores, with hearts of gold, slits of silver, and minds of Einstein formulas. During the summer of 2016, they had paraded a brothel of pathetic babes in front of the Nation's TV cameras to smear and shame Trump out of the campaign. But when their lies about Trump's vulgarity were exceeded only by their lies about the women's virginity and veracity, the whole show shrank to an immediate embarrassing end, like a 2-minute service to a 2000-dollar Weinstein. During 2017 in his first year in office, media clowns screamed President Trump's promised matter-of-fact rejections of more taxes, bureaucracies, trade agreements, climate restrictions would bring about Armageddon, for those who believed in the Bible, and Zombie Apocalypse, for those who did not. When stock markets rocketed to historic highs and jobless rates nosedived to historic lows, media clowns climbed into their clown cars and choked and smoked to all new slapstick silliness. When President Trump became the first President, ever, to actually make some progress on peace and nuclear weapons reductions with communist North Korea, media clowns, with their amoeba sized minds, faked the mushroom cloud gall to criticize President Trump for not being tough enough. These same media clowns had kissed the backsides of all the murderous communist dictators who had ever drenched God's green earth with children's blood.

News faked with forked and funky tongues and fed to all us folks is clearly nothing new. Way back in 1959, Presidents were still permitted to run the country and their Presidencies; sportsmen were still permitted to shoot quail, duck, goose, and pheasant; and restaurants and diners were still permitted to sell real beef steaks with mushrooms and baked potatoes with butter and sour cream, all for $2.00. That is 2 as in 2. Men wore suits and ties, women wore dresses and nylons, and those in between or "outside the box" lounged in local luny bins, and wore straightjackets. Earlier in that year, Bill Paley's CBS television network, the original crackpot communist network, showcased Cuban communist dictatorial whore Fidel Castro on the variety show of American entertainment whore Ed Sullivan. Smooth move that was by founder Bill Paley and his globalist pals to keep CBS on top of the pile, i.e., artistic-political left, or, manure pile. Sullivan's mannequin mannerisms completed a successful early attempt to normalize and profitize drunks, stoners, misfits, beatniks, and lunatics. This demonstrated the second most important purpose of television. CBS did not make Castro shave or wear a pinstriped suit. However, it did make him brush; floss; lose the sewer-stinking stogies, trim his nails and hair on head, ears, nose, and eyebrows; and shower with enough bar soap and afterwards smear on enough deodorant to disinfect the feet, loins, brains, and armpits of every kneeling knucklehead in every NFL and NBA locker room in 2018. Paley and his pals found and paid Hollywood's best Trotsky Stanislavskis and they in turn rehearsed Castro, in between his required bottles of tequila and brothels of prostitutes, a hundred times on voice, tone, pitch, range, body language, eye contact, hand movements, and arm, hip, and leg placements. His brand new pissless, snotless, tearless, bloodless, brainless --- never his but that of his machete-mutilated enemies --- guerrilla fatigues looked as if they had been procured and tailored on Savile Row in London, in between measuring sessions for New World Order Orderlies and Banksters and Gangsters and Their Numb Skull and Boneheaded Commissars. Rehearsing him to an Oscar and Ministry of "Truth" performance, CBS and Sullivan and Khrushchev and Castro performed perfectly the faked improvisational interview. Well paid actors were half the guerrilla fatigues-clad clowns jumping and monkey shining around and behind Sullivan and Castro. For those who were not true card-carrying comrades, it was just another soap opera pay day for sound stage-scampering B-flick lads. Castro promised peace on earth, goodwill toward men, gambling millions for all, democracy, free elections, free daily cigars in every shack, and free nightly rooster fights in every street. Castro seemed as warm, humble, genuine, and neighborly as Saint Paul, Billy Graham, Mr. Rogers, and Captain Kangaroo combined. Those promises broadcast through global networks and those same promises later broken and silenced ever since in the shadows demonstrated the most important purpose of television. As much as the Castros, Maos, Trotskys, Lenins, Stalins of the world, parents of the baby boomers who formulated and boomers who maintained this hell on earth shall take to their afterlife a layer of unscrubbable dirt. God Himself only knows if that layer of dirt also remains irredeemable. Take a good long look at Queen Hillary Artillery's 2016 Mao lookalike outfits. Study fashion trends and fashion history, with scientifically microscopically analytically cold-heartedness. Go back and study Asian political history in exactly the same way. Go back and study Chinese history in the same way. Switch channels, to 1959, to Captain Kangaroo's "sailor" jacket: close the lapels, and sew on a right chest pocket --- and you get the exact same jacket Communist Madman Mao wore when he declared the birth of the People's Republic of China in 1949, one of the most brutal dictatorships in human history. Always remember, that the fake in the fake media empires was test tubed and lab ratted a long long time ago, and not in a galaxy far far away. Kung Fu. Dung Too.

Part II

Infatuation with front door whores has now been replaced by saturation of back door wars. Media circus clowns of the artistic-political left had once again tried, and once again failed, to paint yet another tainted porn star prostitute as some sort of mother earth virgin queen poster child to bring down President Trump. Both for her and for them, the story of their humiliating President Trump into resignation or impeachment ended as stormily as a drop of her venereal-disease-ridden pee in the Mediterranean Sea. The story then dried up faster than a drop of her same pee in the heat of the summer in the Sahara Desert. Hollywood communist male pigs on the casting couches they had manufactured kept poking more holes both in femininity and in their own credibility. And, so, suddenly, President Trump was being hammered from all sides for enforcing border laws, rules, orders, statutes, policies, memorandums, and regulations passed, ordered, enacted, or implemented by former Presidents Obama, Kid Bush, Clinton, Old Bush, Reagan, Carter, Ford, Nixon, LBJ, and JFK. Like fake news, fake borders have been obliterating our Nation for a long time. In the 1960s, for early support for the Vietnam War, LBJ paid off JFK's far left, drunken, hypocritical, Mary Jo Kopechne-murdering brother Ted, by signing a landmark immigration bill that basically marked the beginning of the end of our land as know it. For decades afterwards, at off the record parties and orgies, Camelot black knights and court jesters crowed when drunk and stoned that it was one of Irish Catholicism's best acts of revenge against British Protestantism. That bill drew the blueprints and built the highway robbery roads and highways through the uncontrollable and unaccountable borders of today. More and more laws with each passing decade merely increased the amount of robbery and the number of highways. Even when some conservative Republican Presidents stood smart and tall and tough and dedicated enough to maneuver committed compromises and permanent solutions, liberal Democrat Presidents, Senators, House Reps, and ACLU groups a short time after a law's passage initiated various civil rights challenges in Federal Courts, where activist --- meaning heleter-skelter hyper-active --- Federal judges immediately eliminated the compromises and solutions, as unconstitutional, for which conservatives had battled. Our southern border has become a red carpet for an entirely new breed of international carpetbagger funded, trained, and recruited by vermin like MI-6 operatives, MS-13 drug cartels, the Red Chinese, and the same New World Order Globalists who funded the fake dossier on President Trump. Stinking fake dossier was manufactured by stinking fake public officials and stinking fake human beings. Everywhere there was global camera footage of illegal immigrant mothers and daughters, all obviously overweight, who swam across the widest part of the Amazon River, walked all the way from the rest of Brazil, and swam across the widest part of the Rio Grande River. Yes, they did all of that, but, for interviews with the global media, they could not walk five feet from Government gifted, soft, clean, not-yet-bed-bugged beds. Toddlers fully foreign born with foreign tongues were sobbing "Mommy!" in perfect Elizabethan stage Shakespearean English. They must have benefitted from the same or sons and daughters of the same Trotskied Stanislavski directors, producers, and advisors who tutored Fidel Castro six decades earlier. Teenagers bitter, broken, thirsty, and starving were running around on new playgrounds, shooting hoops, and perfecting power dunks, in their $300.00 per pair LeBron James basketball shoes. That is 3 as in 3 hundred. But, of course, such activities took place only when they were not kneeling for the National Anthem. Or stomping on, or spitting on, or pissing on, or shitting on, the American Flag. Or on Americans. Or burning it. Or Americans.

President Trump is the first America President, certainly since Lincoln, possibly since Washington, who comprehends completely that the President's first duty in making America great once again is making Americans safe, from all enemies, both foreign and domestic. More importantly, President Trump is also the first American Commander-in-Chief, again certainly since Lincoln, again possibly since Washington, who comprehends completely that the President's first place to look is in our own back woods, on our own back roads, in our own back yards, and at our own back doors. The war terminology is apt, since communist nuts on the left started it, way back in the early 1960s, by Jane Fonda, Tom Haden, Jerry Rubin, Abby Hoffman, Bobby Seale, Angela Davis, Bill Ayers, Bernadine Dohrn, Saul Alinsky, H. Rap Brown, and California Governors-to-be Moonbeam Bonehead Brown and Brewsome Gruesome Newsom. Whenever it served their political purposes, they injected race war and ethnic war rhetoric into their class war propaganda. And those still alive and nuts like them still do. Since the 1960s, they have been using slogans like "the war for Latino freedom"; "the fight to feed the children"; "the cry for democracy"; and "the battle for immigration reform." Former law-and-order, America love-it-or-leave-it Presidents on the right like Richard Nixon, Gerald Ford, Ronald Reagan, Old Bush, and Kid Bush; and likeminded loudmouthed candidates like Barry Goldwater, George Wallace, and John Connally; have all spent endless speeches talking tough, but walking small. They were supposed to be the tough guy Presidents, the bone crunchers, and the nut crackers. However, the only things that they ever crunched were numbers at the Fed, UN, and IMF; and the only things that they ever cracked were wall safes, purses, wallets, pay checks, and bank accounts of Great American Middle Class Taxpayers, and rip them off to the point of misery, poverty, and mediocrity. Both Reagan in 1984 and Kid Bush 20 years later in 2004 were elected, specifically, to stop or at least slow the onslaught of illegal immigration. Reagan's half-hearted attempt failed wholeheartedly; Kid Bush's wholehearted absence succeeded wholeheartedly. Since the day when then-Candidate Trump started running and promising to build a wall to stop the drugs, crime, and destruction of the American society and economy, those on the left ramped up the war of words. After five minutes of listening to Emperors McCain, Graham, Rubio, Ryan, Clinton, Obama, Biden, Sanders, and Schumer; and Queens Hillary Artillery, Obama, Pelosi, Feinstein, and Warren, and all their comrades on the artistic-political left, you are slammed by the fact of their insane hatred for this nation in general, and for President Trump and our Great American Middle Class in particular. They have even suckered African House Rep Maxine Waters of Los

Angeles into ordering Trump haters to roam cities and towns and streets and alleys and find Trump supporters and scream and berate and threaten them with harm or death to them and their children.

Fake news fools had not cornered the market on globalist politics of personal destruction. Especially since January 2017, all sorts of other professional socialist losers, flunkies, lunkheads, and meatheads have gotten in on the act, to kick start careers that will never roar down the snake-like road to stardom, or to overhaul careers that will never creakily leave the scrap heap. In England last year former Beatle Paul McCartney, after nearly 64 years of billing, shearing, and feeding on sheep, with salt and pepper, started calling our President Trump crazy for not battling climate change. Now an eternity past primetime, Paul hasn't written a decent song since his Beatle days, and for those he required state of the art subliminal wizardry by warlocks and witches, but he fancies himself some sort of lucid Lucied Shakespeare. Also in England last year, Meghan Markle, Prince Harry's better half but only by a fourth of an eighth, started calling President Trump a divisive pig. She previously in her actress days squealed bit parts as a nurse on soap operas like *General Hospital*, but her pig slop performances in general sent fans to the hospital. She butchered small roles in *Crime Scene Investigation*, but her pig sty performances were deemed criminal and demanded special investigation by Jeff Sessions, our President Trump's goofy agoraphobic AG. And, so, she ran off quite contrary to marry Prince Harry. The latest member of the artistic-political left must have used "divisive pig" since from her swinish standpoint it takes one to know one. Back home in America recently, Samantha Bee, another humorless "comedian" completely consumed by hatred and jealousy of all things and all people normal and successful, screamed insults at and obscenities about President Trump's daughter Ivanka, all of which ended with the C-word. Ivanka is everything that Samantha is not: young, smart, wealthy, beautiful, and powerful.

Rob Reiner is treated as Socrates as actor, director, and activist. He says President Trump is too dumb and unstable to be President. Reiner is 71 and still calls himself Rob as if he were still 7. Like some bumbling Baby Boomers who never grew up, he fell and went kaboom and smashed a gap between his teeth. Basic psychology would conclude he did the same to his brains. Perhaps he is still searching for that elusive endearing fan support earned by his dad, Carl, for Dick Van Dyke for his early 60s sitcom character Rob Petrie. Rob Reiner hasn't directed anything above baloney in 25 years nor acted in anything above baloney in 50 years, but he boasts an ego ballistic enough to blow up the planet. In early 70s he played Meathead in sitcom *All in the Family* and in early 90s directed the movie *A Few Good Men*, but he became never meat, never potatoes, never good, and never a man. Typecast in the former and miscast in the latter, success sprinted away from him, like sanity away from Harvey Weinstein. Rumors swirled Cruise and Nicholson co-directed. Despite 50 years of Reiner's average old man Carl grubbily greasing smuttily sleazy Hollywood palms, along with other particularly lonely loinly parts, Reiner remains lost and strange. His latest flick *Shock and Awe* grossed less than $100,000. Our President Trump is hatefully estimated to be worth only $3 Billion; whereas Reiner, on budget of $150 M, was shocked and awed to learn he made round $3.00. Reiner received a 3 dollar bill, and tried to bank on it. Each day SEC and GAAP mandate that the big dogs at WarnerMedia flip a coin and a Weinstein whore to determine which subdivision, Reiner's Castle Rock, or CNN, will lose more money.

Last but also least, take punky petty Petey Fonda. Please. Take him to Kathmandu. Or take him to Timbukto. Or take him to Babalu. But please just take him. Perhaps take him to the man in the moon, or any other place where others like him do not have a clue, so that the Great American Middle Class, by losers like him, are no longer screwed. Stumblebum son of actor Henry Fonda, younger brothel bum brother of actress Jane Fonda, the punky petty Petey Fonda recently stated, through his Twitter Account, in all caps by the way, that "We should rip Barron Trump from his mother's arms and put him in a cage with pedophiles." Fonda telegraphed that line in reply to the President's enforcement of borders laws in Texas. What a way for the 78-year-old low life loser to refer to The President's 12-year-old son, with more fun and frolic from fools and failures in Follywood. Fonda's justification was that he has been basically and consistently a low life loser for half a century. Of course he tried to walk the comment back but stumbled all over himself and the damage was undeniably done. For most of his crummy career he was able to maintain his political distance from his sister crazy Jane, but that one line made real damn sure that he goes to his cremation with a reputation as some sort of bean pole, pea brained pervert. Like most baby boomers, and like a lot of WWII babies (Stones, Beatles, Grace Slick, Bob Dylan), puny petty Petey will never grow up; his 80-year-old sister will never grow up either; partly because their Follywood fantasy island culture never asked them to; but mostly because their odd ball idiotic old man Henry never required them to. Nobody ever dared discuss the fact that the *Grapes of Wrath* country boy character Henry portrayed was actually in reality light years ahead of Henry intellectually. Ah, yes. Poor dorky homely Henry, who ended his long career pathetically peddling light bulbs on television commercials, never found a way to flip the lights on upstairs when it came to fatherhood. The results were two brats enormously wealthy but irredeemably wacky. Hey, how many actors does it take to screw in a light bulb while filming a movie scene? 500,000. One to hold the light bulb, and the other 499,999 to lift and rotate the sound stage. During the Vietnam War, his sister, aka Hanoi Jane, every other week jetted off to serve and service the Vietcong. Straddling those canons while high on LSD while lusting the Tom Haydens and Leon Trotskys of the world was the only way for the frigid ditz to climax. Her escapades served her well on the sets and in front of the cameras shooting scenes in *Klute* and *Coming Home*, when not able to shoot Americans. Now that history has proven her wrong on everything, without a clue she goes home each day "trying to be happy." Back in 1969, a young, punky, petty Petey made the movie *Easy Rider*. It proudly displayed the American Flag, which he hated then and hated now and hated for the half century in between. The Barron Trump line irrefutably revealed that long hidden fact. That movie made stars out of Nicholson, Hopper, Black, and Harley-Davidson Motorcycles. But not Petey Fonda. Strangely it mutated into his bed time for Bonzo and hot rod for Dumdum. Perhaps his line about Barron was a Lennonesque primal scream. Or Freudian slip. It is important to remember Hollywood did not invent casting couches; it was the other way around, of ten from behind. After all, Hollywood casting couches had always welcomed and cushioned one and all: homo- and hetero-; young girls and young boys; front sides and back sides. Hollywood took great pride in the fact it had perfected not only equal opportunity pedophilia, but also equal opportunity perversity. Hollywood and hypocrisy have always been joined at lips and hips and … Hmm.

President Trump is the first Commander-in-Chief not only to heat the left, but also, and more importantly, to beat the left, at their own games. He comprehends completely you do not have to fly NYC-sized USAF C-5M Super Galaxies nor do you have to sail LA-sized NAVY Trident II Nuclear Submarines halfway around the globe to locate and engage the enemy. War can explode out of nowhere, sneak into your backyard, and break down your back door. That is where we stand right now on our southern border. President Trump knows if we do not stand united then we will fall divided. He knows he has a military duty to use any means necessary to secure our borders and protect American citizens from death and destruction. The left has been calling it a war for 6 decades, whereas President Trump has been calling it a war for a mere 6 weeks. This makes the left heroic, but somehow makes him demonic, among atheists and socialists no less, all without a spec of hypocrisy. The members of the Great American Middle Class know this, and our President Trump especially knows this, but the members of the left do not know that they know, and more importantly do not know that he knows. Arab, African, and Latin American nations, globalists, and governments, concealing their thieves, rapists, terrorists, drug kings, and homicidal maniacs among women and children and sneaking them all into our country, means those nations are declaring war on, and conducting war with, our United States of America. For these nations --- indeed for these continents --- the illegal felons are their ideal warriors. The men are their tanks; the women their howitzers; the children their choppers; and the babies their bombers. Indeed, their suicide bombers. This fear of parents and children being separated is as creditable as the lie that they come here because they love and respect America. The damage inflicted is ten times less costly to those nations and ten times more deadly to our nation. Conservative Commander? Conservative Hero? Reagan was a boot camp private firing blanks compared to the howitzers fired by Commander-in-Chief Trump.

There was no need for President Trump to sign Executive Orders to revise or rescind current or future practices or processes on the borders and in the border wars. He had simply been implementing existing laws, statutes, policies, and regulations, in catastrophically crookedly cooked books. He had already proven himself more compassionate than past Presidents. He was not splitting up Latino families; he was splitting up Dummycrat hypocrisies. He was not snatching offspring from Latino moms and dads; he was snatching drug kings from American towns and roads. He was not sending Latino children to internment camps; he was sending illegal felons through exit ramps, and back to the nations that had transformed them into mindless mercenaries. Members of artistic-political left wanted to look cute and called illegal felons "caged"; many patriots and nationalists on the right wanted to look correct and called illegal felons "mercenaries." Since day one, President's Trumps message has been very clear, very direct, and very simple: if you do not want to be "caged" in any way, then do not cross our borders illegally. Very clear, very direct, and very simple. But the New World Order wolves in lambs clothing kept telling illegal felons to cross our borders illegally and so they did and so they still do. They came and they came and they came and they keep coming and keep coming and keep coming. They do not know they are global pawns in a global chess match. They do not know they are war materials and beasts of burden to be bought or sold and won or lost and stamped or branded in a global game of New World Order monopoly. They are the bombs, bullets, and grenades. Where are Peter, Paul, and Mary? Where are Slick, Dylan, and Lennon? Where are all the WWII babies and baby boomers and their sons and daughters in wedlock and out of wedlock to storm Mexico City to conduct anti-war protests? To listen to the lunacy by those who own and control the artistic-political-parasitic left, it is all the fault of minimum wage white guys who swing hammers at construction sites, or turn wrenches at ruck and auto plants, or white moms who stay at home and change their babies' diapers and their toddlers' pajamas. Illegal felons have been poor, sick, homeless, and luckless, almost their entire lives. They do not know the reason is their corrupt and drug cartel-bribed rulers. Their rulers tell them it is America, and they should go to the border and sneak in and "take back by any means necessary what Americans have stolen from them since the days of the Alamo." America is the reason the fathers have no work to earn;

their wives have no food to cook; their children have no shoes to wear; and their babies have no milk to drink. Of course they sneak in. Of course they are caught. When they are, for the first time, mothers and their children enjoy hot meals, hot coffee, hot chocolate, and hot clean parasite-free water; cold ice cream, cold ice tea, cold soda, cold real milk, and cold real butter; new clothes, new shoes, soft beds, and warm blankets; roofs without leaks, rooms without rats, and playgrounds without drug lords. All Free. All without Thanks. Not courtesy of 13 past Presidents. But courtesy of President Trump acting on behalf of the Great American Middle Class Taxpayers who elected him and have supported him and remain royally loyal to him.

Children have been decorated, denigrated, separated, or eliminated from families and communities; for cultural, religious, military, and political purposes; since the very first day; of the very first family. Cain and Abel, the offspring of Adam and Eve, had barely bounced past puberty when older brother Cain murdered younger brother Abel. The feud of blood and flood of blood was so bad that the screams of Abel's blood soared from earth to Heaven to God. So it began. After invading the no longer promised land, God's no longer chosen people, those murdering hordes of murmuring morons, drenched the desert sands with human blood, obliterating anything that breathed, beginning with babies. Ancient Hebrew parents, elders, authorities, rulers, and kings, methodically marched disobedient children out beyond their village gates, tied them up, and stoned them to death. Those are just two reasons, out of hundreds, that Jesus came to earth and generally vilified some of their leaders as generations of vipers. Not to be outdone, Egyptian, Philistine, Babylonian, and Persian empires, when not their own children, captured children of their enemies, i.e., the Jews among others, and roasted them alive in fire pits as sacrifices to their demon gods. Greek and Roman empires not only perfected war, math, and science; but they also perfected homo- and hetero- drunken orgies with young boys and young girls. Muhammed told members of his empire Allah told him these practices of other empires were permissible, with girls as part of marriage; ever since, Arab men have sliced up their women as they next hour sliced up goat cheese, lamb chops, and chicken breasts. Asian and African men would tightly bind the feet of girls and young women, not because small feet were a sign of beauty, but because young women were highly prized spoils of war, like horses or weapons or gem stones, and they had to be prevented from escaping. Including "mature" Mexico, modern African and Latin American nations have established 12 years of age as consent for sexual relations. Young women have no idea what a penis even is until it pierces their virginity, like a Goliath-sized spear. All this cave man crap is called cute. If you scan fake news reports in that rag of record NYT, or fake news stories on that smut of record CNN, each one will tenderly refer to 35-year-old boneheaded bums playing video games 24/7 in their parents' basement, and 35-year-old college indoctrinated clowns, paid millions, at start of their NFL games kneeling in protest, as "youngsters." Cain the tiller of soil probably sharpened a broken lamb bone from the flocks of Abel the keeper of sheep. Cain gutted Abel in the same way Abel gutted his sheep, or Latino MS-13 "youngsters" 1000s of years later machete-gutted American gringos, or Radical Arabian-islamic Terrorists (RATs) "youngsters" 1000s of years later stiletto-flayed vulvas of American infidel women, all in the name of Gold, Silver, Mother Mary, Father Allah, Seeds of Truth, and Loads of Laughs.

There was a time when numbers did not lie. There was a time when numbers did not twist, omit, distort, or interfere with truth, wisdom, reality, or history. There was a time when 6 days of God's work and 1 day of Sabbath rest equaled 7 days for the Creation process. There was a time when for 2 plus 2 equaled 4, E equaled MC squared, and death was the only certainty in life, not high taxes. That time is long gone and permanently gone, along with scrolls, ink wells, carbon paper, and manual typewriters. The numbers of separated illegal alien children from illegal alien parents have always been distorted or unconfirmed or manufactured or pulled out of thin air, in the same way the last three Democrat President stooges, meaning Jimmy Peanut Butter Brain, Bill Bonehead, and Oh Bonehead, jerked fake "successes" of their Presidencies out of fake global warming, goblin gobbling thin air. For the same reasons, distortions have gone in the other direction, on the number of illegal immigrants already here and contributions they already make to the American economy. For years fake college and fake media empires have stated around 10 – 12 million maximum, with all working hard, and all paying taxes. Without them, the entire American economy would collapse. And Google, Yahoo, Facebook, Twitter, Tweeter, Pumpkin, and Eater never censor anyone. The last three sentences are more fake news. Based on the standard arithmetic of addition, subtraction, division, and multiplication, the true number is 25 – 30 million minimum. That is based simply on verifiable federal, state, and local public assistance records and government budgets. In most New York, Florida, Texas, and California grade, middle, and high schools, English is the second language, and sometimes the third. Most of these illegal alien parents work their minimum wage jobs and feed their maximum dole loins, meaning have 4 – 5 children, where the annual cost to educate one child for one year is an extremely easily verifiable $12,000 - $16,000 (that comes from hard left teacher unions, who are always striking or clamoring for more money). In California alone the current State education budget is $80 Billion and the State welfare budget is another $100 Billion. The nuts on the left have given a whole new catastrophic meaning to the term "fun with numbers." Conservatives' fuzzy math? Socialists' blurry algorithms come straight from twilight zones and outer limits. They have almost always owned and controlled the next sign post, the next stop light, all that we see, and all that we hear. The $64 Billion question that has never been asked nor investigated is: If all are working hard, and all are paying taxes, why cannot they be found, and deported? But back to the border wars, the numbers of these children are verifiably fake; just like those of starving children during the Kid Bush years were verifiably fake; of homeless adults during the Old Bush and Reagan years were verifiably fake; of seniors without winter heating during the Ford years were verifiably fake, and of jailed and beaten anti-war protesters during the Nixon years were verifiably fake. However, numbers that are neither distorted nor unconfirmed nor manufactured nor plucked out of the backsides of fake reporters and fake professors all favor President Trump. Polls indicate that media approval is way down and that President Trump's approval is way up. Few polls stating otherwise are the same "scientific" polls that stated Hillary would beat Bernie in 2016 in Michigan, before Bernie buried her by 30 points, and that she would pound Trump into dirt by 5 – 15 points. The only accurate poll was Investor's Business Daily, who had him alternately winning or losing by 1 or 2 points. Numbers of up close camera shots of separated children have vanished. Why? They are wearing brand new designer shirts, shorts, socks, and sometimes $100 Nike shoes, feasting on meat and vegetables, gulping milk, and spooning ice cream with cake, off clean plates, on clean tables, and in clean facilities, all without any thanks, all paid for by Great American Middle Class Taxpayers, all of whom must work, twice as hard, twice as long, and twice as smart, to provide the same luxuries for their own children.

It is both bizarre and bewildering to behold Queen Hillary Artillery, Bill Bonehead, Oh Bonehead, and Joe Bonehead; college, media, and internet empires; and their Christianity-crucifying communist commissars and comrades, quote from the Bible. Almost all of them are fakes and phonies, almost all of them are atheists and agnostics, and the number of their lies and hypocrisies is exceeded only by the number of grains of sand in the Earth's deserts. To catch Queen Hillary quote from the Bible on the border wars is to watch her moron of a husband Bill Bonehead preach on the respect for women he and other globalist socialist pigs supposedly hold deep within their hearts and souls. They are all wolves in lamb's clothing and they are all the ones about whom the Good Lord warned us. As with WWII camps and abortions, only in 21st century America could modern cosmopolitan globalist socialists get away with preaching to various Christians and proving them on Jesus Christ, His New Testament, His Truth, His Wisdom, His Crucifixion, and His Resurrection. All Jews, Sunni Moslems, Shiite Moslems, Hindus, Buddhists, Earth-Worshippers, Satan-Worshippers, and Outer Space Alien-Worshippers have always been extremely clear, direct, and to the point on the fact that their religious beliefs, principles, and practices apply only to fellow believers. To lie, to spy; to distort, to misdirect; have always been perfectly permissible methods for conversion or destruction of enemies and infidels.

And when conversion was not and is not a success, then subjection and destruction were and still are commandments. The only times she and her husband, former Putrident, er, President, no, Putrident, Bill Bonehead hauled around Bibles from Which to quote were the times hard-core power politics demanded it. Back in the 1990s, while he was pretending to be an American President, being impeached, and whoring around with White House intern Monica Lewinsky, and dozens of floozies in dozens of cities, and outright raping other women like Paula Jones, Gennifer Flowers, Kathleen Willey, and Juanita Broaddrick, and doing his best JFK beltway and below the belt impersonations, Bonehead and Hillary made out like bull manure bulldozing bandits. In fact, ever since, that money-grubbing pair has made out like money-changing thieves, in a den of thieves, in a house of prayer, or in a temple, at some tables, that were overturned --- by The Lord. The Gospels of Matthew, Mark, Luke, and John recorded that episode of personal confrontation and spiritual purification as the only time on this Earth that He became exasperatingly angry and explosively fire-and-brimstone violent. Hillary Artillery never even tried to lie, but Bill Bonehead lied every time he said "God bless America," but he did not lie when he took his wonky winnings to the nearest bank and signed his name on the deposit slip, and the banksters did not lie when they took, and were more than happy to take, that pair's windfall winnings. Thomas Jefferson certainly was politically prophetic when he stated banking institutions were more dangerous than standing armies. Ever since, at parties and gatherings on the right, a coin flip game was often played, with an one-ounce pure gold double eagle coin: heads that pair gave more Swiss banks secret cash to Ross Perot to steal votes from Old Bush, or tails that pair gave more of the same to Old Bush to toss votes down the drain. During their shared Putridency, he and she instructed the media empires to carefully and dutifully lock the cameras on them, so that they could always be seen around the globe with Bibles that outweighed the 25-pound Kenneth Starr Impeachment Report on Bill Bonehead by an additional 25 pounds. That is why years ago she stopped saying "God bless America"; that is why she lost the Democrat race to Oh Bonehead in 2008; and that is why she lost the Presidential race to our President Trump in 2016. Hillary's endless attempts to re-invent herself over the years have always failed. That is also why her it-takes-a-village theme to convey compassion for children failed. Everyone knows that when she talks about a village, except for her most intimate comrades and commissars, she thinks everyone else constitutes a bunch of village idiots.

Recently Queen Hillary Artillery converted to the theology of amnesty and to the economy of money growing on trees. She pulled on her Hollywood designer sheep's clothing to become a globalist socialist soldier in the borders wars, mostly in the form of Mao jackets. Oh, sure, poverty was a virtue, but there was no need to go Essene to the extreme. Since the late 1960s, permanently babied baby boomers like her had quoted from Matthew 19. Hillary Artillery has attacked so much lately in so many speeches on the border wars. She bragged so much about her Methodist background, Sunday school teacher days, and supposed expertise on both Old Testament and New Testament, that you would think she was channeling not only her inner Eleanor Roosevelt but also her inner Mother Teresa. Hillary omitted the fact both Old and New condemn such heresy as the work and the power and the incarnation of demons. As always, out of context, she quoted the early Matthew chapter 19 verses, about how Jesus suffered the little children to come to him and to listen to him, for the kingdom of heaven consists of them. As always globalist socialists like her who want cheap labor illegal foreigners --- and their votes --- are angels, whereas various conservatives who do not are devils. It is worth noting once again that, at this point prior to His Crucifixion and Resurrection, His Laws, Truths, Wisdom, and Salvation applied mainly to other Jews, and to very few exceptions that He had made, such as the Good Samaritan and Roman Centurion. He had not yet commanded His eleven disciples to go and teach all nations, baptizing them in the name of the Father, and of the Son, and of the Holy Ghost. The primary point of His instruction in Matthew 19 had nothing to do with borders, since the Jews, to secure and maintain their own borders, had waged wars with foreign armies for 4,000 years. His primary point was that adults needed to be as true and honest and open-minded as children in the pursuit of Heaven and Salvation, as opposed to Egyptian, Babylonian, Persian, Greek, Roman, and Jewish laws, customs, traditions, and theologies. His secondary point was that children indeed should leave their parents and follow Him, if the parents were idiots and idolaters, the blind leading the blind, the Numb Skulls leading the Numb Skulls, and the Bone Heads leading the Bone Heads.

Part III

Last week it was front door whores. This week it is back door wars. Always massaged every month is a new flavor, savory, and slavory. Next week, who knows. Perhaps it will be barn door chores, and how Trump's forcing wheat, corn, and dairy farmer parents to send their 5-year-olds out in the fields to harvest crops, or castrate bulls, by hand, by themselves. Perhaps it will be black door oars, and Trump's forcing Blacks, Homos, Lesbos, and Latinos into FEMA camps at night, then to seaports, to row row row their boats, to Africa. Or perhaps it will be trap door floors, and how Trump's forcing boomer seniors to build hidden basements and secret rooms and helter-skelter shelters to hide their children's children from Trump's Stormtroopers. Boomer hidden Swiss tax shelters and offshore Caribbean bank accounts have already been perfunctorily put in place. It only took a few villages (and a few village idiots) propped like mannequins in store fronts to fool half the planet into thinking Clintons and others made all those trips to Europe to glad hand the globalists about global warming. Or perhaps it will be Supreme Court camp fire smores, and how Trump's forcing the Supreme Court to become the supreme law of the land Bible belt, Chastity belt, and ancient Roman Empire Scourging Belt. But, underneath these new flavors, there is always the plain vanilla of free and open doors and rampaging assembly line amnesty for all illegals, and how Trump's forcing millions of them into FEMA camps, and forcing them to conform. Oh. Wait. Leftists already do that. They call it public education. In Shakespeare's day, boys were castrated to keep their voices high like women, and painted up to play women parts. Prostitution in all forms has always been only the world's second oldest profession. Separation of children from families in all forms has always been, in fact, the world's oldest

Our Commander-in-Chief and President, Donald Trump, is the first one, certainly since Lincoln, possibly since Washington, to focus on the fact that the most important wars explode out of nowhere, on your country roads, on your city streets, in your back yards, and at your back doors. Kid Bush, hiding behind his Mephistophelian Fake twang, like LBJ and JFK before him, and Truman and FDR before them, plunged our Nation in yet another far off war on yet another far off part of the planet. That war in sands dry and barren has become an upside down inside out quicksand of American tears and blood. That war to destroy weapons of mass destruction has become nothing but wastelands of lost delusions. That lousy stinking war stole arms and legs and minds and souls of America's best and brightest and bravest and strongest. That lousy stinking war served to preserve the New World Order of Banksters and Fake Media Empires and Bilderbergers and Bohemian Grovers and Boneheads. Under Kid Bush during the early days of the New World Order's latest war, members of the artistic-political left in major cities would snatch street people, grab homeless drunks and mindless druggies, stick protest signs in their hands, and make them march around to show "massive anti-war" solidarity in front of fake news cameras. Common nonsense on signs said "No Blood for Oil" and "Death to War Pigs." What was never reported then or now is that the members of our Great American Middle Class never received any free oil, or any free pork chops, or any free lamb chops, or any free desert sand, or any free anything. Tightwad estimates of the total cost under Kid Bush and Oh Bonehead was 5 Trillion dollars. If you throw in Oh Bonehead's 11th hour flights of fancy and red eye flights to Iran by military cargo planes crammed to crashing with U.S. and other currencies, you are up to 7 Trillion. If you total since the 1960s the astronomical costs for shelter, clothing, food, water, schools, colleges, health care, legal services, not only for illegals stopped at the border, but also, and more importantly, for illegals who came in and stayed in and free loaded in, you must multiply that by 10.

History does not record if God spent 10 trillion dollars per day or 10 cents per day for the 7 day cycle for His Creation of the heaven and the earth. History does not record if He had to comply with IRS laws and SEC regulations, doubling the cost. History does not record if He had to utilize wind, solar, and electric trucks, dozers, and graders, tripling the cost. History does not record if He had to complete beetles, spotted owls, global warming studies, and global climate assessments, quadrupling the cost. History does not record location of the Ten Commandments; nor the Ark of the Covenant that held them; nor 100,000 talents of gold that went into construction of Solomon's

Temple; nor 1,000,000 talents of silver that went into construction of Solomon's Temple. History does not record location of the cup that Christ used at His Last Supper; nor of the 30 pieces of silver paid by Jewish jackasses to Judas for His last betrayal; nor of the wooden cross to which He was nailed; nor of the Roman spear which pierced His side.

However, history does record, and God only knows for how long until he is wiped Orwellianly out of the books of earth's history, the first real President, and the first real Commander-in-Chief, to provide and advance the first real solutions to the front door whores and the back door wars: Donald J. Trump.

News: Walls: Newspapers: Wallpapers:

From the first day of the Garden of Eden to the last day of the End of Days, God reminds us many times in many ways that there will always be walls. As long as there are Heaven and Hell, Christ and Satan, Good and Evil, Angels and Demons, Salvation and Perversion, Ambition and Perdition, Time and Space, Love and Hate, Life and Death, Truth and Myth, Wisdom and Sodom, stars and moons, sun and earth, oceans and mountains, inventers and preventers, producers and reducers, makers and takers, sealers and stealers, choosers and boozers, there will be walls. In the real world, in the true universe, this will always be both perfectly normal and perfectly natural. God's Word, from beginning to end, reminds us all of this eternal fact:

As stated in the 3rd Chapter of the Book of Genesis:
Thorns also and thistles shall it bring forth to thee; and thou shalt eat the herb of the field; In the sweat of thy face shalt thou eat bread, till thou return unto the ground; for out of it wast thou taken: for dust thou *art*, and unto dust shalt thou return. And Adam called his wife's name Eve; because she was the mother of all living. Unto Adam also and to his wife did the LORD God make coats of skins, and clothed them. And the LORD God said, Behold, the man is become as one of us, to know good and evil: and now, lest he put forth his hand, and take also of the tree of life, and eat, and live for ever: Therefore the LORD God sent him forth from the garden of Eden, to till the ground from whence he was taken. So he drove out the man; and he placed at the east of the garden of Eden Cherubims, and a flaming sword which turned every way, to keep the way of the tree of life.

And as stated in the 21st Chapter of the Book of Revelation:
And he carried me away in the spirit to a great and high mountain, and shewed me that great city, the holy Jerusalem, descending out of heaven from God, Having the glory of God:

and her light *was* like unto a stone most precious, even like a jasper stone, clear as crystal; And had a wall great and high, *and* had twelve gates, and at the gates twelve angels, and names written thereon, which are *the names* of the twelve tribes of the children of Israel: On the east three gates; on the north three gates; on the south three gates; and on the west three gates. And the wall of the city had twelve foundations, and in them the names of the twelve apostles of the Lamb. And he that talked with me had a golden reed to measure the city, and the gates thereof, and the wall thereof. And the city lieth foursquare, and the length is as large as the breadth: and he measured the city with the reed, twelve thousand furlongs. The length and the breadth and the height of it are equal. And he measured the wall thereof, an hundred *and* forty *and* four cubits, *according to* the measure of a man, that is, of the angel. And the building of the wall of it was *of* jasper: and the city *was* pure gold, like unto clear glass. The fifth, sardonyx; the sixth, sardius; the seventh, chrysolite; the eighth, beryl; the ninth, a topaz; the tenth, a chrysoprasus; the eleventh, a jacinth; the twelfth, an amethyst. And the twelve gates *were* twelve pearls; every several gate was of one pearl: and the street of the city *was* pure gold, as it were transparent glass. And I saw no temple therein: for the Lord God Almighty and the Lamb are the temple of it. And the city had no need of the sun, neither of the moon, to shine in it: for the glory of God did lighten it, and the Lamb *is* the light thereof.

This historian attended schools, colleges, and universities when fundamental arithmetic, mathematics, algebra, and geometry were still functional, rational, logical, and rocket scientifically sound. In other words, they had not yet been climatically changed nor globally warmed, as in cooked text books, as in fried computer programs, as in Fahrenheit 451 scorched facts of heart and truths of mind and laws of nature into floating swirling blackening ash. Back then Hinterland teachers, instructors, and professors demanded, dictatorially, of me, and all of us, simply as a starting point to earning a "C" on report cards, that students "show their work." The exception of course had always been anytime a Kennedy ran for a National office. Especially the Presidency. As reinforced resoundingly since page one of this volume, the New World Order and their Deep Staters and their Orderlies and their Disorderlies and their Borderlesslies and their priorities and their slaveries and their Ivy League methodologies for their deliberate destruction of the Great American Middle Class, have been around a long time, at least since the assassination of President John F. Kennedy, and perhaps since the assassination of Abraham Lincoln. That exception has been expanded exponentially over the decades to include all Dummycrats and all offices and all levels. Even San Fran-Cess-Pool poop mapper. In those special instances, it then simply took, and now simply takes, a small village and available village idiots not only to raise the children but also to count the votes. This historian is ready and willing and able to show the work --- more dutifully and more eternally God's handiwork. Far beyond bizarre how the full-of-rum Tweedledumber than dumb freemasons are able to maintain all that Solomon's Temple Hiram Horse Manure Nonsense as a 500-year-old publicity stunt, but have ignored the Law, and the Truth, and the Wisdom, and the Knowledge of God's Word. Sickeningly secretive freemasons mapped out Washington, D.C., as a Pentagram in honor of their Luciferian masters. It was no accident equally sickeningly secretive freemasons mapped out the Pentagon almost 200 years later.

At Christ's Second Coming, God's Holy City, New Jerusalem, will be a perfect square with all sides equal. Please note the ancient measurement of the furlong. Ancient Math --- God's math: natural math: normal math --- states that there are eight furlongs in one mile. So, 12,000 divided by 8 = 1,500 Miles. This is fairy tales according to the New World Order and their fake media empires. But let us add nuts and bolts and steel and concrete. Please find a map of the North American Continent. Start in our Nation's Capital, which is Washington, D.C., which is toxically swamped with the New World Order's creepiest Deep State drunks and cronies and flunkies who are the ones responsible for all the hell on Earth since World War I and the constant political assassination attempts on our President Trump.

From Washington, DC, go 1,500 miles west to Denver:
Then go 1,500 miles south to Mexico City:
Then go 1,500 miles east to Jamaica:
Then, lastly, go 1,500 miles north back up to DC.
This constitutes both width and length.
The height of New Jerusalem will stretch the same 1,500 miles straight up.
Please note shortest distance from Earth to space is 62 miles.
Please note most satellite operations stop at 100 miles
Please note International Space Station (ISS) orbits at 254 miles.
New Jerusalem will rise 1,246 miles higher than ISS.
And, finally, there are the walls.

Yes, there will be walls to define and detail and support the majestically massive and massively majestic structure. Walls will be 144 cubits thick. Tribes of Israel 12 multiplied by Apostles of Christ 12 equals 144. God's point here is that both groups are needed, and both Old and New Testaments are needed, to make the Bible whole and complete. Depending on culture and society, in the ancient world, cubits ranged from 17 to 23 inches. To give to God all honor and glory for all He has created, we will assume the long royal cubit of 23 inches. So 12 multiplied 12 equals 144. 144 cubits multiplied by 23 inches equals 3,312 inches. 3,312 divided 12 equals 276 feet. An Official U.S.A. NFL Football Field is 100 yards long, or 300 feet long. Therefore, the walls of God's New Jerusalem will be almost the length of an NFL field thick. Even an unrepentant and unapologetic and undeniably damned Darth Vader would be forced to admit soberly: "Most Impressive," but he would whisper the words in a tone of horrific fear and foreboding, on both knees, with head bowed. Almost all Americans know these NFL fields. They are the fake media empires' seeded fields of treasonous weeds where knock-kneed, knock-boned, knock-brained knuckleheads kneel before games to display their hatred for the fans who have and Nation which has been so good to them. In light of these facts, it is easy to see at the start of 14th Chapter in the Gospel of John both how and why Jesus could state:

> Let not your heart be troubled: ye believe in God, believe also in me. In my Father's house are many mansions: if *it were* not *so*, I would have told you. I go to prepare a place for you. And if I go and prepare a place for you, I will come again, and receive you unto myself; that where I am, *there* ye may be also.

Unlike the time of His First Coming in Bethlehem near the old Jerusalem where there was no room at the inns, at His Second Coming, for those who accept him as the Way and the Truth and the Life, and as Lord and Savior and only begotten Son of God, there will be plenty of rooms, and, at 1,246 miles higher than ISS, plenty of room. Reservations can be made anytime anywhere. And you don't need face books, cell phones, computers, or credit cards. Wow. Talk about admirable. Talk about affordable. Talk about available; Talk about undeniably customer friendly. Enough talk. Recommend doing so. Here. Now.

In the end, at the end, as long as there are men and women, as God has both defined them and created them, with faith in The Holy Trinity, and men and women with faith in gold, silver, brass, and iron; as long as there are men and women, as God has both defined them and created them, with faith in The Holy Trinity, and men and women with faith in globalism, socialism, atheism, and hedonism; and, finally, as long as there are men and women, as God has both defined them and created them, with faith in The Holy Trinity, and men and women with faith in earth, air, water, and fire, there will be walls.

The New World Order's New Smokestack America

(Hint: Not Commie Nut Jobs Burning Forests in Cali-Commie-Pornia)

There once was a Nation

So Beautiful … so Plentiful … so Dutiful … so Heavenly Blessed

That even cosmic creatures and big-footed beasts

From here to Alpha-Centauri … were impressed

But deeply and stately and worldly and orderly and borderlessly came

With their jim crow and karl marx and empires and vampires and opioids and aspartames

Now all us Citizens who Spent Our Lives to Pray and Sweat and Slave and Aspire

Are under Air … and under Earth … and under Water … and under Fire

And under house and home and mouse and chrome and grouse and dome arrest

Moreover boned and droned and phoned and stoned and comatose arrest

When they are not enslaving or incinerating us and our spouses and our children and our grandchildren and our friends and our Bibles

For fun … for profit … for misfits … for pests … in jest … …

Federal Reserve Serves Nation's Fiscal Calamities

(In the following Federal Case Law, all highlights, er, lowlights, are this historian's)

(Yes, that same far left nut case Ninth Circuit which has declared that President Trump and Middle Class American Taxpayers are the scum of the earth, and that bugs and weeds and creeps and freaks and illegals and terrorists and the New World Order's drug lords and war lords and slum lords and overlords, and the global money-changing lords that bankroll and profiteer from them all … are the salt of the earth)

680 F.2d 1239

John L. LEWIS, Plaintiff/Appellant,

v.

UNITED STATES of America, Defendant/Appellee.

No. 80-5905.

United States Court of Appeals,
Ninth Circuit.

Submitted March 2, 1982.
Decided April 19, 1982.
As Amended June 24, 1982.

Lafayette L. Blair, Compton, Cal., for plaintiff/appellant.

James R. Sullivan, Asst. U. S. Atty., Los Angeles, Cal., argued, for defendant/appellee; Andrea Sheridan Ordin, U. S. Atty., Los Angeles, Cal., on brief.

Appeal from the United States District
Court for the Central District of
California.

Before POOLE and BOOCHEVER,
Circuit Judges, and SOLOMON, District
Judge.*
POOLE, Circuit Judge:

On July 27, 1979, appellant John Lewis was injured by a vehicle owned and operated by the Los Angeles branch of the Federal Reserve Bank of San Francisco. Lewis brought this action in district court alleging jurisdiction under the Federal Tort Claims Act (the Act), 28 U.S.C. § 1346(b). The United States moved to dismiss for lack of subject matter jurisdiction. The district court dismissed, holding that the Federal Reserve Bank is not a federal agency within the meaning of the Act and that the court therefore lacked subject matter jurisdiction. We affirm.

In enacting the Federal Tort Claims Act, Congress provided a limited waiver of the sovereign immunity of the United States for certain torts of federal employees. United States v. Orleans, 425 U.S. 807, 813, 96 S.Ct. 1971, 1975, 48 L.Ed.2d 390 (1976). Specifically, the Act creates liability for injuries "caused by the negligent or wrongful act or omission" of an employee of any federal agency acting within the scope of his office or employment. 28 U.S.C. §§ 1346(b), 2671. **"Federal agency" is defined as:**

the executive departments, the military departments, independent establishments of the United States, and corporations acting primarily as instrumentalities of the United States, but does not include any contractors with the United States.

28 U.S.C. § 2671. The liability of the United States for the negligence of a Federal Reserve Bank employee depends, therefore, on whether the Bank is a federal agency under § 2671.

5

There are no sharp criteria for determining whether an entity is a federal agency within the meaning of the Act, but the critical factor is the existence of federal government control over the "detailed physical performance" and "day to day operation" of that entity. United States v. Orleans, 425 U.S. 807, 814, 96 S.Ct. 1971, 1975, 48 L.Ed.2d 390 (1976), Logue v. United States, 412 U.S. 521, 528, 93 S.Ct. 2215, 2219, 37 L.Ed.2d 121 (1973). Other factors courts have considered include whether the entity is an independent corporation, Pearl v. United States, 230 F.2d 243 (10th Cir. 1956), Freeling v. Federal Deposit Insurance Corporation, 221 F.Supp. 955 (W.D.Okla.1962), aff'd per curiam, 326 F.2d 971 (10th Cir. 1963), whether the government is involved in the entity's finances. Goddard v. District of Columbia Redevelopment Land Agency, 287 F.2d 343, 345 (D.C.Cir.1961), cert. denied, 366 U.S. 910, 81 S.Ct. 1085, 6 L.Ed.2d 235 (1961), Freeling v. Federal Deposit Insurance Corporation, 221 F.Supp. 955, and whether the mission of the entity furthers the policy of the United States, Goddard v. District of Columbia Redevelopment Land Agency, 287 F.2d at 345. Examining the organization and function of the Federal Reserve Banks, and applying the relevant factors, we conclude that the Reserve Banks are not federal instrumentalities for purposes of the FTCA, but are independent, privately owned and locally controlled corporations.

6

Each Federal Reserve Bank is a separate corporation owned by commercial banks in its region. The stockholding commercial banks elect two thirds of each Bank's nine member board of directors. The remaining three directors are appointed by the Federal Reserve Board. The Federal Reserve Board regulates the Reserve Banks, but direct supervision and control of each Bank is exercised by its board of directors. 12 U.S.C. § 301. The directors enact by-laws regulating the manner of conducting general Bank business, 12 U.S.C. § 341, and appoint officers to implement and supervise daily Bank activities. These activities include collecting and clearing checks, making advances to private and commercial entities, holding reserves for member banks, discounting the notes of member banks, and buying and selling securities on the open market. See 12 U.S.C. §§ 341-361.

Each Bank is statutorily empowered to conduct these activities without day to day direction from the federal government. Thus, for example, the interest rates on advances to member banks, individuals, partnerships, and corporations are set by each Reserve Bank and their decisions regarding the purchase and sale of securities are likewise independently made.

It is evident from the legislative history of the Federal Reserve Act that Congress did not intend to give the federal government direction over the daily operation of the Reserve Banks:

It is proposed that the Government shall retain sufficient power over the reserve banks to enable it to exercise a direct authority when necessary to do so, but that it shall in no way attempt to carry on through its own mechanism the routine operations and banking which require detailed knowledge of local and individual credit and which determine the funds of the community in any given instance. In other words, the reserve-bank plan retains to the Government power over the exercise of the broader banking functions, while it leaves to individuals and privately owned institutions the actual direction of routine.

H.R. Report No. 69, 63 Cong. 1st Sess. 18-19 (1913).

The fact that the Federal Reserve Board regulates the Reserve Banks does not make them federal agencies under the Act. In United States v. Orleans, 425 U.S. 807, 96 S.Ct. 1971, 48 L.Ed.2d 390 (1976), the Supreme Court held that a community action agency was not a federal agency or instrumentality for purposes of the Act, even though the agency was organized under federal regulations and heavily funded by the federal government. Because the agency's day to day operation was not supervised by the federal government, but by local officials, the Court refused to extend federal tort liability for the negligence of the agency's employees. Similarly, the Federal Reserve Banks, though heavily regulated, are locally controlled by their member banks. Unlike typical federal agencies, each bank is empowered to hire and fire employees at will. Bank employees do not participate in the Civil Service Retirement System. They are covered by worker's compensation insurance, purchased by the Bank, rather than the Federal Employees Compensation Act. Employees traveling on Bank business are not subject to federal travel regulations and do not receive government employee discounts on lodging and services.

12

The Banks are listed neither as "wholly owned" government corporations under 31 U.S.C. § 846 nor as "mixed ownership" corporations under 31 U.S.C. § 856, a factor considered in Pearl v. United States, 230 F.2d 243 (10th Cir. 1956), which held that the Civil Air Patrol is not a federal agency under the Act. Closely resembling the status of the Federal Reserve Bank, the Civil Air Patrol is a non-profit, federally chartered corporation organized to serve the public welfare. But because Congress' control over the Civil Air Patrol is limited and the corporation is not designated as a wholly owned or mixed ownership government corporation under 31 U.S.C. §§ 846 and 856, the court concluded that the corporation is a non-governmental, independent entity, not covered under the Act.

13

Additionally, Reserve Banks, as privately owned entities, receive no appropriated funds from Congress. Cf. Goddard v. District of Columbia Redevelopment Land Agency, 287 F.2d 343, 345 (D.C.Cir.1961), cert. denied, 366 U.S. 910, 81 S.Ct. 1085, 6 L.Ed.2d 235 (1961) (court held land redevelopment agency was federal agency for purposes of the Act in large part because agency received direct appropriated funds from Congress.)

14

Finally, the Banks are empowered to sue and be sued in their own name. 12 U.S.C. § 341. They carry their own liability insurance and typically process and handle their own claims. In the past, the Banks have defended against tort claims directly, through private counsel, not government attorneys, e.g., Banco De Espana v. Federal Reserve Bank of New York, 114 F.2d 438 (2d Cir. 1940); Huntington Towers v. Franklin National Bank, 559 F.2d 863 (2d Cir. 1977); Bollow v. Federal Reserve Bank of San Francisco, 650 F.2d 1093 (9th Cir. 1981), and they have never been required to settle tort claims under the administrative procedure of 28 U.S.C. § 2672. The waiver of sovereign immunity contained in the Act would therefore appear to be inapposite to the Banks who have not historically claimed or received general immunity from judicial process.

15

The Reserve Banks have properly been held to be federal instrumentalities for some purposes. In United States v. Hollingshead, 672 F.2d 751 (9th Cir. 1982), this court held that a Federal Reserve Bank employee who was responsible for recommending expenditure of federal funds was a "public official" under the Federal Bribery Statute. That statute broadly defines public official to include any person acting "for or on behalf of the Government." S. Rep. No. 2213, 87th Cong., 2nd Sess. (1962), reprinted in (1962) U.S. Code Cong. & Ad. News 3852, 3856. See 18 U.S.C. § 201(a). The test for determining status as a public official turns on whether there is "substantial federal involvement" in the defendant's activities. United States v. Hollingshead, 672 F.2d at 754. In contrast, under the FTCA, federal liability is narrowly based on traditional agency principles and does not necessarily lie when the tortfeasor simply works for an entity, like the Reserve Banks, which perform important activities for the government.

16

The Reserve Banks are deemed to be federal instrumentalities for purposes of immunity from state taxation. Federal Reserve Bank of Boston v. Commissioner of Corporations & Taxation, 499 F.2d 60 (1st Cir. 1974), after remand, 520 F.2d 221 (1st Cir. 1975); Federal Reserve Bank of Minneapolis v. Register of Deeds, 288 Mich. 120, 284 N.W. 667 (1939). The test for determining whether an entity is a federal instrumentality for purposes of protection from state or local action or taxation, however, is very broad: whether the entity performs an important governmental function. Federal Land Bank v. Bismarck Lumber Co., 314 U.S. 95, 102, 62 S.Ct. 1, 5, 86 L.Ed. 65 (1941); Rust v. Johnson, 597 F.2d 174, 178 (9th Cir. 1979), cert. denied, 444 U.S. 964, 100 S.Ct. 450, 62 L.Ed.2d 376 (1979). **The Reserve Banks, which further the nation's fiscal policy, clearly perform an important governmental function.**

17

Performance of an important governmental function, however, is but a single factor and not determinative in tort claims actions. Federal Reserve Bank of St. Louis v. Metrocentre Improvement District, 657 F.2d 183, 185 n.2 (8th Cir. 1981), Cf. Pearl v. United States, 230 F.2d 243 (10th Cir. 1956). State taxation has traditionally been viewed as a greater obstacle to an entity's ability to perform federal functions than exposure to judicial process; therefore tax immunity is liberally applied. Federal Land Bank v. Priddy, 294 U.S. 229, 235, 55 S.Ct. 705, 708, 79 L.Ed. 1408 (1955). Federal tort liability, however, is based on traditional agency principles and thus depends upon the principal's ability to control the actions of his agent, and not simply upon whether the entity performs an important governmental function. See United States v. Orleans, 425 U.S. 807, 815, 96 S.Ct. 1971, 1976, 48 L.Ed.2d 390 (1976), United States v. Logue, 412 U.S. 521, 527-28, 93 S.Ct. 2215, 2219, 37 L.Ed.2d 121 (1973).

18

Brinks Inc. v. Board of Governors of the Federal Reserve System, 466 F.Supp. 116 (D.D.C.1979), held that a Federal Reserve Bank is a federal instrumentality for purposes of the Service Contract Act, 41 U.S.C. § 351. Citing Federal Reserve Bank of Boston and Federal Reserve Bank of Minneapolis, the court applied the "important governmental function" test and concluded that the term "Federal Government" in the Service Contract Act must be "liberally construed to effectuate the Act's humanitarian purposes of providing minimum wage and fringe benefit protection to individuals performing contracts with the federal government." Id. 288 Mich. at 120, 284 N.W.2d 667.

19

Such a liberal construction of the term "federal agency" for purposes of the Act is unwarranted. Unlike in Brinks, plaintiffs are not without a forum in which to seek a remedy, for they may bring an appropriate state tort claim directly against the Bank; and if successful, their prospects of recovery are bright since the institutions are both highly solvent and amply insured.

20

For these reasons we hold that the Reserve Banks are not federal agencies for purposes of the Federal Tort Claims Act and we affirm the judgment of the district court.

AFFIRMED.

Well, well, well …

In summary, the Court, by denying Mr. Lewis a lousy 64 Hundred Dollar vehicle injury settlement, inadvertently resolved the 64 Trillion Dollar question of the 21st century.

The Federal Reserve System since its monstrous creation in 1913 has been the deepest and most secretive and most sinister and most unstoppable of all Deep State institutions, not only in America but also around the globe, from the streets of Milwaukee to the streets of Nagasaki to the streets of Budapest, Hungary.

The fact that the Federal Government has never exercised any fundamental control over the "Federal" Reserve System, on a day-to-day basis, or week-to-week basis, or month-to-month basis, or year-to-year basis --- or for that matter decade-to-decade basis --- is exactly the Ninth Circle of Hell problem.

Never underestimate the power of the New World Order's Commissars and Deep Staters and orderlies and disorderlies and borderlesslies and drunks and punks and flunkies, not only when they are boozing and whoring in backwoods cabins at Bohemian Groves, but also, and more importantly, when they are babbling and rambling from court room benches in black robes.

To Understand Strange Blood

From a book written exactly one century earlier:

… …

It is no easy task to understand strange blood …

… …

I want to have goblins about me, for I am courageous. The courage that scares away ghosts creates goblins for itself --- courage wants to laugh …

… …

It is true: we love life, not because we are used to living, but because we are used to loving.
There is always some madness in love. But there is always also some reason in madness.
Friedrich Nietzsche
Thus Spoke Zarathustra

Coffee Break

Sir Valentine:

These banish'd men that I have kept withal

Are men endued with worthy qualities:

Forgive them what they have committed here

And let them be recall'd from their exile:

They are reformed, civil, full of good

And fit for great employment, worthy Lord.

… …

The story of your loves discovered:

That done, our day of marriage shall be yours;

One feast, one house, one mutual happiness

(*Two Gentlemen of Verona.* 1594. V. IV. 2310 – 2315;
2329 - 2331).

Hmm …

Love … from Sir …

Love … from Spear Shaker …

From Verona … To Milan …

Re Avon … N Mail …

Re Nova … N Mail …

Hmm …

Yes … …

God IS our refuge and strength, a very present help in trouble. Therefore will not we fear, though the earth be removed, and though the mountains be carried into the midst of the sea; THOUGH the waters thereof roar AND be troubled, THOUGH the mountains shake with the swelling thereof. Selah. THERE IS a river, the streams whereof shall make glad the city of God, the holy PLACE of the tabernacles of the most High. God IS in the midst of her; she shall not be moved: God shall help her, AND THAT right early. The heathen raged, the kingdoms were moved: he uttered his voice, the earth melted. The LORD of hosts IS with us; the God of Jacob IS our refuge. Selah. Come, behold the works of the LORD, what desolations he hath made in the earth. He maketh wars to cease unto the end of the earth; he breaketh the bow, and cutteth the spear in sunder; he burneth the chariot in the fire. Be still, and know that I AM God: I will be exalted among the heathen, I will be exalted in the earth. The LORD of hosts IS with us; the God of Jacob IS our refuge.

Psalm 46 1-11
KJV

Then said Martha unto Jesus, Lord, if thou hadst been here, my brother had not died. But I know, that even now, whatsoever thou wilt ask of God, God will give IT thee. Jesus saith unto her, Thy brother shall rise again. **Martha saith unto him, I know that he shall rise again in the resurrection at the last day. Jesus said unto her:** I am the resurrection, and the life: he that believeth in me, though he were dead, yet shall he live: And whosoever liveth and believeth in me shall never die. Believest thou this? **She saith unto him, Yea, Lord: I believe that thou art the Christ, the Son of God, which should come ...**

**John 11: 21-27
KJV**

The End